The Madcap Christian Scientist:
All Things New
by Karen Molenaar Terrell

For Rachael –
with much love –
infinite love!
Karen

For Marilyn, Marla, Bev, and Lori,
Xander, Andrew, and Scott, Pete and Dave,
Moz and Dad, and for the people of my
"tribe" – you know who you are. I am so
very blest to know you.

*Her world had turned abruptly
upside down and tipped her out of it ...*
- Douglas Adams

*They have only two possible
messages. The first is an automatic response
to the second, and the second is an
automatic response to the first. The first is,
"Here I am, here I am, here I am." The
second is, "So glad you are, so glad you are,
so glad you are."*
– Kurt Vonnegut

*"It isn't like that at all; it isn't like
building - not a bit. In building, you see, you
know beforehand what it's going to be
like ...I mean, it would never do to start off
building a house and find you've built a
bridge, or something, when it was all
finished. It's more like hunting, really,"* said
Barbara, *warming up to her subject. "...It's
an adventure, you see, that's the beauty of it.
You don't know a bit what you're going to
find until you come to the end, and, even
then, you don't know what you've found."*
- D.E. Stevenson

Behold, I make all things new.
- Revelation

Vonnegut, Stevenson, and Adams
Talking in My Head

In the beginning, God created the earth, and he looked upon it in His cosmic loneliness. And God said, "Let Us make living creatures out of mud, so the mud can see what We have done." And God created every living creature that now moveth, and one was man. Mud as man alone could speak. God leaned close as mud as man sat up, looked around, and spoke. Man blinked. "What is the purpose of all this?" he asked politely. "Everything must have a purpose?" asked God. "Certainly," said man. "Then I leave it to you to think of one for all this," said God.

- Kurt Vonnegut

But our early man has a moment to reflect and he thinks to himself, "Well, this is an interesting world that I find myself in," and then he asks himself a very treacherous question, a question that is totally meaningless and fallacious, but only comes about because of the nature of the sort of person he is, the sort of person he has

1

evolved into, and the sort of person who has thrived because he thinks this particular way. Man the maker looks at his world and says, "So who made this, then?" Who made this? - you can see why it's a treacherous question. Early man thinks, "Well, because there's only one sort of being I know about who makes things, whoever made all this must therefore be a much bigger, much more powerful and necessarily invisible, one of me, and because I tend to be the strong one who does all the stuff, he's probably male."

And so we have the idea of a God. Then, because when we make things, we do it with the intention of doing something with them, early man asks himself, "If he made it, what did he make it for?"

\- Douglas Adams

Beloved, let us love one another: for love is of God; and every one that loveth is born of God, and knoweth God. He that loveth not knoweth not God; for God is love... God is love; and he that dwelleth in love dwelleth in God, and God in him.

I John 4

This year I've had the great good privilege of holding conversations with authors Douglas Adams (author of *The Hitchhiker's Guide to the Galaxy* series), Kurt Vonnegut (author of *Slaughterhouse Five* and other equally amazing novels), and D.E. Stevenson (author of the *Miss Buncle* books). Okay, so I didn't, like, actually *talk* to any of them in the person – seeing as how they're all dead and everything, but I did have the great joy of reading their books for the first time this year, and sort of… well… talking to them in my head.

We all laughed together at the nonsense of life and humankind and ourselves, we chatted about God, and I found kinship with them in our similar views of "Life, the Universe, and Everything" (another of Adams's books).

Adams and Vonnegut were atheists (I didn't find any place in her writings where Stevenson actually voices her thoughts regarding a belief in God) and, although I *do* believe in God, I, too, am an atheist when it comes to an anthropomorphic god who lives in the clouds and zaps his children to hell periodically. I am of the opinion that THAT kind of a god should have long ago gone the way of Zeus and Mars and ridden off into the sunset on his fiery chariot never to be seen again except in the study of ancient cultures and literature.

I wish I would have found Adams, Vonnegut, and Stevenson earlier in my life. I can't believe it took me so long. I'm sad that I didn't get to know Adams – who was only five years older than me – when he was walking the earth. I'm sad that his sudden death at the age of 49 didn't have the significance to me that it would have, had I known him then. I wish I would have understood, then, what his early departure meant to the world. And when I read his last book, *The Salmon of Doubt* – compiled in the year after his death by his friends and editors – I found myself sobbing when I got to the end of it – knowing there wouldn't be any more. I felt like I had lost a good friend.

Kurt Vonnegut introduced his readers to the fictitious but way cool religion of Bokononism in his book, *Cat's Cradle,* and I will be making periodic references to Bokononism in my book.

And D.E. Stevenson introduced me to the wonderfully enlightened and wise Miss Buncle, who's brought me laughter and the comforting feeling that I am not alone as I pretend to be a grown-up.

I'm going to bring my new friends into this book with me. They are a part of my life now, and they need to be a part of this book, too.

Starting New

I seldom end up where I wanted to go, but almost always end up where I need to be.
– Douglas Adams

She had new friends, who valued her for what she was and accepted her as she was; and she had new interests which increased and multiplied daily.
- D.E. Stevenson

We'd all do well to start over again, preferably with kindergarten.
- Kurt Vonnegut

It's only been two years since I sent *The Middle Book* out into the world, and I'm pretty sure that this isn't "The End Book" here – so maybe we can think of this one as "The Second Middle Book"?

In The Second Middle Book I find myself unboxed. Unplugged. Unfettered. (No, no - not unhinged. Mostly.)

Two years ago I would never have been able to guess where I'd be today, what

6

I'd be doing, and what new people I would be calling my friends and colleagues. Two years ago my youngest son was close to graduating from high school, my 20-year career as a public school teacher was winding down, and I was looking for a new job and a new purpose to fill my days. Two years ago I was starting over.

It was scary. It was exhilarating. It was absolutely awesome!

For the first time in years I didn't have to try to fit my life into a rigid schedule and a tight structure. My life was my own to create as I felt led. Creativity danced up to the front of the line - opportunities that required my skills and talents as a writer presented themselves, and photography became a big part of my life. Concerns with conformity, pleasing others, and financial security retreated to the rear.

And I had a sort of epiphany: I never want to be paid so much money that I no longer own my own "soul." I want enough to live and be comfortable and to share with others – but I don't want so much that I become dependent on it, and feel the need to give up my own sense of right and wrong to keep getting it. I never, again, want to feel beholden to a company or business or system, for my security. I never again want to feel owned or boxed. I want what I do to matter – not because it makes me money, but because it gives my life meaning.

I remember clearly a moment when I was twenty-five and had my first job as a teacher with a year-long contract. There was a golf course next to the school where I worked, and I remember one day, as I was pulling out of the school parking lot, I glanced over and saw a couple of older retired gentlemen happily swinging golf clubs and moving along the course in a relaxed, unhurried way. They looked so comfortable with themselves – so content and settled and happy. I remember thinking that these were men who had lived through the Great Depression, served in World War II, or maybe the Korean War – they'd survived life-and-death struggles in their lives – and there was probably little that could scare them, anymore. They'd gotten to a place in their lives where they no longer panicked about what the future might hold.

And I hoped that one day I would have their wisdom, their confidence in life, their lack of fear and panic about the future.

I think I am finally making some progress in that direction.

The Great Escape

And then there is the money cycle.
You're paid a lot and you're not happy, so
the first thing you do is buy stuff that you
don't want or need— for which you need
more money."
– Douglas Adams

You didn't do the easier thing; you
did the thing that would give the more
pleasure.
- D.E. Stevenson, from *Miss Buncle*
Married

The summer before I left my public
school career I'd serendipitously run into an
amazing woman named Laura who owned
and ran an alternative high school in
Bellingham – a city about twenty miles to
the north of me. When I met her she had just
learned that the funds she'd been expecting
from her local school district for the new
school year had been pulled. She wasn't sure
she was going to be able to continue running
her program. But she invited me to come to
a meeting at the school and meet the rest of

the staff. I went to the meeting and was really impressed by what I saw there. Although, sadly, the school was forced to close soon after the meeting, my brief encounter with Laura had opened my eyes to a whole 'nother world that existed outside the traditional classroom. I saw a school where the students' unique gifts were nurtured, where their individuality was valued, where the teachers knew each and every one of them by name, where there was no pressure to fit students into some kind of mold, or put them together on an assembly line. It gave me hope.

Maybe that's when I began to recognize that I'd be willing to exchange my public school teacher's salary and benefits for a lesser salary if I could feel that what I was doing as a teacher was meaningful and had purpose.

By the time I met Laura I was feeling almost desperate to escape the public school system. The workings of public education had brought me some major disappointment and a fair amount of frustration the last half of my career – mandates that made no sense, curriculum that changed overnight, student

11

assessments that didn't test what teachers had been ordered to teach, inefficient use of training and skills, classroom management programs that were too rigid and didn't work for every teacher in every situation, a system that was punitive rather than encouraging for students and teachers – in short, a system that had been taken over by politicians and corporate executives whose goal for students seemed to be to prepare them to fit into a corporate workforce. The creativity, spontaneity, and fun teaching moments were being eliminated from teaching and replaced with scripts and a bunch of acronyms - one administrator actually told me that I needed to stop doing all "those fun things" I did with the students - and he referred specifically to the Night of the Notables - where students researched an historical figure and then, in costume, played the part of that person for one night - and inviting in a Holocaust survivor to share her story with my class - "we" no longer had time for those things in a public school classroom, he'd told me.

It seemed to me that the more teachers got paid, the more insane became the hoops that teachers and their students were forced to jump through, and the more obvious it became that teachers were viewed as property, rather than a valuable public resource. The school district's thought seemed to be, "We pay you. We own you."

I did not want to be owned. But how much was I willing to pay to buy back my freedom? And… did I have the courage to leave a place of financial security to launch myself into The Great Unknown?

I'll be honest, I am not especially brave.

What made the situation really difficult for me wasn't so much concern about myself, but concern about my family. I had a son in university and another about to graduate high school, a mortgage to pay, and groceries to buy – there were people I loved depending on me. As Paulo Coelho writes in his book, *The Alchemist*, "We know what we want to do, but we are afraid of hurting those around us in order to pursue our dream." But he continues, "We do not realize that love is just a further impetus, not something that will prevent us going forward. We do not realize that those who genuinely wish us well want us to be happy and are prepared to accompany us on that journey."

I was deeply unhappy with my career – the disconnect between what the district wanted me to do, and what I knew was right for my students was causing a lot of inner conflict and turmoil for me - and it was changing me into a stressed, cranky, depressed woman. How could that possibly be a good thing for the people I loved?

Early in the new school year I saw that an old friend of mine was substituting as principal for the day at the school in which I worked in the morning. I ran into him in the copy room and asked him if he wouldn't mind talking with me for a few minutes. He said sure, and invited me into the principal's office. I shared with him my feelings about my career, and asked him what advice he could give me about how to make the transition out of public education, should that time come for me. Oh man. He was so helpful! I know I was meant to talk with him that day. His wife had made the transition out of public education just the year before, and he knew exactly what steps I needed to take to extricate myself from my career if and when that time should come. He walked me through the process, step-by-step, while I took notes.

My plan – if I had any – was to hold on to my career as long as I could, in the hopes that something would change – that it would all somehow get better, and I'd be able to continue teaching. And I maybe could have limped along in that career for years, if, in the end, circumstances hadn't become absolutely unbearable for me. In the end, leaving was a no-brainer. And, in retrospect, I'm really grateful that things got unbearable.

I hadn't expected to leave my job so soon. But because I'd felt led a couple months earlier to talk to my financial advisor, and had happened to have the conversation with my friend, the principal, everything was already, weirdly and fortuitously, in place for me when I made the final break. I hadn't been consciously preparing to quit. But, without being consciously aware of it, some part of me was doing what needed to be done for myself in a most effective and efficient way.

Coming to My Senses

*He had never envisaged the
possibility of spring getting lost (so to
speak).*
- D.E. Stevenson

*It is a mistake to think you can solve
any major problems just with potatoes.*
– Douglas Adams

*Many people desperately need to
receive this message: "I think and feel much
as you do. care about many of the things you
care about, although most people do not
care about them. You are not alone."*
– Kurt Vonnegut

In *The Madcap Christian Scientist's
Middle Book* I make mention of my Year of
Insanity – the year I turned 51 and had the
Perfect Storm of a clinical depression. That
year was a really intense life-changing one.
I'm glad it happened. I'm also really glad
it's over.

During the Year of Insanity I hadn't
taken any medications or sought out

17

professional help to deal with the mental illness – I'd felt it was something I needed to work through on my own, and I didn't see how talking about it was really going to help. And, looking back, I'm sure my instincts were right about that. I give credit to the understanding of God, Love, that I'd gained through Christian Science for getting me through the Year of Insanity. I learned so much from that time. It forced me to be aware and conscious of the beauty in each moment – made me a better artist and a more empathetic person to others. That year helped me discover how strong I actually am.

I went through another period of depression as I was transitioning from the public school system at the age of 55 – this time the depression was completely brought on by extrinsic factors, rather than from something inside me. I was diagnosed by the family physician as suffering from severe anxiety and depression, and he recommended I take Prozac. I asked him if I could, instead, see a counselor to deal with the depression – and he agreed to prescribe counseling sessions for me.

In order to find a counselor I had to call my health insurance's mental health line. That was kind of scary for me, but I was sane enough to know that I needed to do this for myself. The woman on the other end of the line was very nice and asked me a series of questions. One of the last questions she asked me was if I'd considered suicide in the last week. That might have been the hardest question I've ever had to answer in my life. "Yes," I admitted. She asked me if I'd planned how I would do it. "Yes," I told her. She asked me what method I'd come up with. "A semi-truck," I said. She asked me why I hadn't done it, "Because I am a chicken," I said. "I was scared. It might hurt, and I really don't like pain." She started laughing then – and I really appreciated that she was able to see the humor of it with me – and she told me it was a good thing that I didn't like pain and that I'd been scared – those were good signs. She gave me some names of counselors I might choose from, and I picked a woman named Jennifer.

When I called Jennifer's office and talked to her receptionist I learned she wasn't just a counselor, she was a psychologist. That seemed pretty serious to me. I told her receptionist that maybe I should go to someone else because I wasn't so bad that I needed a psychologist, I just needed a counselor. The receptionist asked if she could have Jennifer call me before I made any decisions, and I said yes.

When Jennifer called she explained that a psychologist was just the same as a counselor except she had a doctor's degree. That seemed alright then, and I made an appointment.

Jennifer was really great. I'd never done any kind of counseling before and wasn't sure what to expect, really – but Jennifer made the whole experience painless for me. She gently prodded me to find out what it was I needed and wanted to change in my life, and how I was going to do that. She helped me see that I wasn't in a hopeless situation, but that I had options. She didn't tell me what to do, but she helped me discover for myself what it was I needed to do to bring sanity to my life. She helped me find a vision for my future – helped me discover what things were most important to me, and what things were making me insane. She helped me find the courage to bring more of the good things into my life, and to kick the insane stuff out of my life.

The first time we met I mostly sat there and blubbered to her about the dysfunction of my job – the crazy mandates, the lack of support, the feeling that I was being set up for failure. And Jennifer just let me pour it out without interruption. The second time we met I told her about the directive I'd been given to fix things in my job that it was impossible for me to fix – and that's when Jennifer quietly asked me, "Do you plan on going back to this job?" That question caught me up short. I told her I didn't really see how I could. "Then why," she asked me, "are you spending energy worrying about fixing something you don't have to fix?"

Whoah, right?

That was a moment of epiphany for me. At that moment I was able to let go of all the nonsense of my career and start looking forward to something new – the nonsense was not my problem anymore. With Jennifer I began to construct what my future might look like, if I could design it for myself. It would include time to go on walks and take photos and sit and think and write and create. There would be freedom. There would be laughter and joy. There would be purpose and meaning and useful doings.

During this time I also discovered Laura LaVigne, director of the Center for Happiness in nearby Anacortes (my financial advisor is actually the one who recommended I check out her Center). I went to a Vision Board workshop and created a board with pictures symbolizing what I wanted for myself in the next year – concentrating not on any specific form it would take, but on the essence of it – and I pasted down pictures that showed freedom, joy, courage, peace, integrity, and love.

A New Job

*"The worst thing that could possibly
happen to anybody," she said, "would be to
not be used for anything by anybody."*
– Kurt Vonnegut

*It was a great relief to find that
somebody wanted her, that she was not
utterly and completely useless.*
- D.E. Stevenson

*Zaphod tried to run in several
equally decisive directions simultaneously.*
- Douglas Adams

So an interesting thing happened
when I left the public school system: I
realized I actually loved teaching!
I was surprised to find out how much
I missed working with young people -
seeing the expression on the face of a
student when she learns something new;
hearing the laughter of my students; being
revitalized by their energy. I missed
nurturing my students' strengths and gifts,
and helping them gain confidence in their

ability to solve problems they didn't think they could solve. Now that I was out of teaching, and had the opportunity to step back and look at my career from some distance, I realized how much I'd loved the teaching part of it, and how good I actually was at it.

I had no desire to return to a public school setting, but I started mulling over other teaching possibilities – maybe I could tutor students? Or… work at a children's museum? Or… teach in some kind of after-school program?

I needed to find work – not just for the income (although that was important), but because I needed a sense of purpose – I needed to feel I was useful.

While I was working my way out of one job and into the next, one of the authors I found really helpful for me was a man named Edward A. Kimball, who had been a Christian Science lecturer and teacher in the early 1900's. In his book, *Lectures and Articles on Christian Science*, Kimball writes, "It is probable that there will come a time when you will be in quest of professional or business occupation; when you will be in want of a situation. Let us assume that you will be entitled to it and that it will be right for you to be employed righteously and profitably. Such an assumption as this carries with it scientifically the conclusion that if it is right for you to have such a thing, that thing must be in existence and must be available… One of the most influential human conditions is the one which I will call expectancy… You are entitled to the fullness and ampleness of life, but you will need to learn that gloomy foreboding never solves a problem and never releases the influences that make for your largest prosperity and advantage."

I returned to this passage over and over during the last couple years of my public school career, and even more in the months after I left it.

Finding myself unemployed was a new adventure for me. I'd been teaching almost all of my adult life, and I hadn't had to look for work for 20 years. Weirdly, I didn't feel panicked about finding another job – it had become really obvious to me that God was leading me where I needed to go, and I trusted that She had something prepared for me. I just opened myself up to all the infinite possibilities, and waited to see what would happen next.

And all kinds of things happened next: My church gave me the job of librarian at the Christian Science Reading Room and paid me a small salary to manage it; A friend told another friend who worked for an educational publishing company about my teaching background and experience as a writer, and I got a contract to proofread and write some material for the company; I put together some notecards of my photos and started selling them at a little coffee shop in a town nearby; My book, *Blessings: Adventures of a Madcap Christian Scientist*, was bringing in a small amount in royalties every month. Although I wasn't getting a LOT of income – it was really no more than a *symbolic* income, I guess - it was enough to give me some confidence in the future.

One afternoon, when I was just a few months away from resigning from the school district, I found myself sitting next to the mother of one of my son's friends at a high school cross-country meet that our sons were both running in. As we began to converse with each other, I realized I was meeting a new friend. Kim was really smart, with a wonderful sense of humor, and she had a lot of the same interests as me. When she asked me about my current situation, we compared notes about our experiences with the local school district, and found we had another thing in common – similar thoughts on the state of public education. She looked at me for a moment, a thoughtful expression on her face, and said, "You know, I think you would fit in really well at the alternative high school where I work." It turned out that Kim was the co-director of a non-profit organization that provided support and services for families and teens, and the other co-director, Janice, was in-charge of an alternative high school that was under the umbrella of this same non-profit. Kim suggested I stop in and introduce myself.

I filed Kim's suggestion away in the back of my mind, and didn't give much thought to it for several months. During that time I wrote a book about teaching, wrote the *Middle Book*, started serving one day a week at the Christian Science Reading Room, got elected as a delegate to the state Democratic convention, got involved with the Happiness Sprinkling Project created by Laura LaVigne… and officially quit my teaching job.

But at the end of May - on my way to pick up my oldest son from university for summer break - I remembered my conversation with Kim, and impulsively stopped by the alternative school to see if there was a job application available.

I expected to be there maybe 15 minutes, but ended up staying an hour. Janice came out of her office and introduced herself. She gave me a history of the school, a tour of the building, introduced me to the staff and some of the students, and provided me with an application. When she learned that I was going to be traveling to Alaska in July, she told me to check in with her after I got back to see if there were any job openings.

When I got back from Alaska I found an email waiting for me from Janice, saying she'd like to meet with me. I contacted her and we scheduled a time for me to come in and talk with her.

I was nervous. I thought I was going to a job interview, and - I cannot help myself - I always get a little nervous about that kind of thing. What kinds of questions should I be prepared to answer? Should I know a bunch of educational acronyms? Should I be prepared to talk about my management style? Would she ask me that question about my strengths and weaknesses? What should I wear?

But when I got there Janice didn't really ask me any questions. She seemed a little embarrassed, and most concerned, about the reality that this was a non-profit organization and couldn't pay me what public school teachers make. After she'd apologized about salary for the third or fourth time, I finally understood! – "Are you offering me a job?" I asked, starting to get excited. "Yes, but we can't pay..." Janice started to say again, but I interrupted her. "Oh! I don't care about the money! If you're offering me a teaching job, I'll take it!"

And so began a new chapter for me. Within a few months of leaving the public school system, I had found another teaching job – the best job I had ever, ever had! - working with students one-on-one, teaching everything from social studies to geometry to photography – and even helping to chaperone the students on a two-night-three-day snowshoe trip on Mount Baker my first winter there. (Yeah – I got paid for snow-shoeing. How cool is that?!) I was doing work that was meaningful, purposeful, and helpful to young people, and working with a group of colleagues who were dedicated to the teaching profession, and enjoyed teaching for the same reasons I did. I was having fun.

I couldn't have gotten into this teaching position if I hadn't been willing to leave the other position. Quitting the other job put me in a mental place that made me open and available to all the possibilities "out there". It gave me the freedom and time to explore fresh paths and meet new people, and it put me in a position where I'd be ready and able to leap into something new when the moment came.

You know that old saying about quitters never succeeding? I am here to tell you that sometimes having the courage to quit the course you're on and head off into a different direction is the absolutely best thing you can do for yourself.

Alaska

And all dared to brave unknown
terrors, to do mighty deeds, to boldly split
infinitives that no man had split before...
- Douglas Adams

Peculiar travel suggestions are
dancing lessons from God.
- Kurt Vonnegut

And above all, watch with glittering
eyes the whole world around you because
the greatest secrets are always hidden in the
most unlikely places. Those who don't
believe in magic will never find it.
– Roald Dahl

For a very long time I had wanted to visit Alaska. I can't remember when, exactly, the thought had come to me that I'd like to travel up the Inside Passage, visit Mount Denali, look at glaciers, and see grizzly bears and caribou and Native villages – but it was there. With my public school teaching career coming to a close – and the salary that came with it - the idea of going on any kind of vacation to any place further than 300 miles away might have appeared to some to be out of our financial reach.

But when has a little financial shortage ever stopped Good from happening?

I married into a wonderful family. My husband, Scott, has three younger sisters who are now my sisters, too. One of them, Beverly, majored in marine biology, teaches tai chi and swim exercise classes at her local YMCA, and lives outside of Pittsburgh with her anesthesiologist husband, Matt. And one day we got a call from Bev asking us if we'd like to join Scott and Bev's mom, Marilyn, Bev's husband, and their son, Jordan, on a trip to Alaska. They, she said, would pay for the entire trip. (!) (Matt said, "Why would we invite you on a trip with us and then expect you to pay?" I love him.)

Bev organized the whole thing for us through her favorite travel agency – flights to Anchorage, train and bus rides to get us into Mount McKinley National Park, and a bus ride to the Alaskan coast, where we would board a cruise ship and travel through the Inside Passage to Vancouver, Canada.

I was nervous about the cruise part, to tell you the truth. Whenever I'd thought of traveling through the Inside Passage I'd pictured myself roughing it on the ferry that travels from the Puget Sound to Alaska - sleeping in a sleeping bag under the stars with the briny smell of saltwater filling my nostrils, and the sounds of seagulls filling my ears. For some reason, I'd never pictured myself as a passenger on a cruise ship, sleeping in a room with no access to the air outside. I was feeling a little leery about that part – I'm kind of claustrophobic. I worried, too, that if I didn't have access to fresh air I might get seasick - several summers before I'd been a passenger on a double-hulled hydro-ferry from Portland, Maine to Nova Scotia, Canada, and it had not gone well for me - diesel fumes and really big waves had knocked me out for the count.

Another thing that was making me nervous about the cruise was the warning that if we felt we were coming down with some kind of contagious anything we should be responsible human beings, report ourselves immediately to a doctor, and not get on the ship and expose other hapless individuals to our illness. For some reason, my thoughts had gotten snagged up on all the possible problems that might arise if I got sick – what if I got sick and couldn't get on board the cruise ship? How would I get back home? And… and… what if I got sick and GOT on board the cruise ship and made everyone else sick? And… and… what if I had to report myself to a doctor and then ended up quarantined for the entire week?! Yeah. Have I mentioned that I'm a little neurotic?

It's probably not surprising that the day we caught our flight out from Seattle to Anchorage I felt myself coming down with a cold. Sniffles. Sneezing. Fever. (Fear.)

It was weird to arrive in Anchorage late at night and sill be walking around in daylight. But it was a good kind of weird.

Early the next morning, we set out to see the sights of Anchorage. We were immediately captivated by the profusion and brilliant colors of the flower beds scattered throughout the city - Anchorage maybe doesn't get a whole lot of sunshine and light for much of the year, but when summer comes the gardeners of Anchorage don't waste a minute of it - the city runs ariot with the color of begonias, lupines, and foxglove planted in every available inch of city space. We bought reindeer hot dogs from a lovely young woman from South America who travels to Alaska every summer to work the reindeer hot dog stand, and ate the hotdogs while we watched a kids' soccer game. It was fun to chat with the parents at the game, and to realize that being a "soccer parent" in Anchorage is no different than it is in Seattle – there was the same excitement when a child scored his first-ever point, the same laughter when the youngest players all bobbed along the field in one exuberant clump, the same "ooh" and "ah" when the goalie stretched out horizontal and stopped the ball from entering the net. It was a reminder that the joys of parenthood are universal.

From Anchorage we headed by bus to the Grizzly Bear Lodge - a clean, woodsy little motel that sits on the edge of a happily babbling creek and lies close to the entrance of Denali National Park. The next day, Don, our tour bus driver, chauffeured us 62 miles into the park and up to a viewpoint of Mount McKinley - highest mountain in North America. We'd been cautioned by everyone we met that the odds of actually seeing the mountain are 3 in 10. But I had absolutely no doubt that we'd see McKinley – and sure enough, the clouds shifted, and we did! The land in front of McKinley was permafrost tundra, dotted with scrubby little bushes – and McKinley rose straight up out of the tundra – it was hard for me to wrap my brain around the hugeness of it. As I scanned its vast expanse, I felt connected to my dad, Dee Molenaar, who had traveled to McKinley to help rescue his friends, the Whittaker twins, from its slopes when I was a young girl.

Driving through the park we were blest to sight grizzly bears, a couple moose, an Arctic fox, and some caribou amongst the bushes and snowfields, and even some doll sheep moving around on the mountain ridges. It was a spectacular day!

The next day we traveled to a wildlife rehabilitation center, and the starting point for the Iditarod dogsled race. Then, faces licked and fingers gnawed by lively blue-eyed puppies who would one day race in the Iditarod, and cameras full of the images of rehabilitated moose, bears, and caribou, we boarded the Millennium cruise ship to embark on the nautical part of our Alaskan adventure.

My cold had gotten worse. My ears were clogged, my nose was running and red, and I had a fever.

As we made our way up to the cruise ship security and customs people to have our luggage checked and to be admitted onto the ship, I was nervous the security folks were going to look at my runny nose and ask me if I was sick. Being the conscientious, honest – and did I mention I'm neurotic? – individual I am, I wasn't sure I'd be able to tell them with a clear conscience that I felt completely fine if they asked.

No one asked.

But when we got to our room we found a note waiting for us, telling us that there was a problem, and we needed to report to the customs and security room to pick up our luggage in-person.

I thought I was busted – that they must have noticed my red nose and sniffles when we'd passed through security, and were now going to have me escorted off the ship for the good of humanity.

I was really scared – have I mentioned that I'm a little neurotic? - and asked Scott to pick up the luggage for us because I did not want to go down to the cruise ship catacombs. But he had something else he had to take care of, so, my stomach in knots, I got in the elevator and hit the button that would take me to, like, the bottomest bottom of the ship.

When I got off the elevator I saw a long line of people waiting to claim their luggage. This was surprising. Was everybody busted for having the sniffles? I asked the security lady what was going on, and was told that most everyone had purchased Ulu knives – knives that the

Native peoples used for skinning animals, and chopping vegetables and blocks of ice. She asked me if I'd purchased one, and I told her no. But when she unzipped my bag there were three of them sitting right on top! How the heck did THOSE get in there?! The security lady was very nice and told me I could claim the Ulu knives at the end of the cruise, then she gave me my luggage and told me there was nothing more I needed to do there. I wasn't going to get thrown off the ship for my sniffles after all!

(As it turns out, Scott had purchased the Ulu knives and hadn't told me.)

Once I realized that I wasn't going to get kicked off the ship, I started feeling better right away. I finally put some thought into getting a healing for myself. Mary Baker Eddy writes in the Christian Science textbook, "Destroy fear, and you end fever." And so it proved for me. I sang hymns to myself, wrapped myself up in Love and joy, and claimed nothing but Good as my experience – and not only MY experience, but the experience of every single person on board that boat. Good, I told myself, is contagious, and I was going to do my part to spread it all over that cruise ship.

The next day our cruise ship brought us up-close to the Hubbard Glacier. Having been raised by a mountaineer, I have climbed around on glaciers almost all my life – I've climbed to the tops of Rainier and other glaciated mountains in the Pacific Northwest – but the Hubbard Glacier absolutely took my breath away. It was simply magnificent – bright turquoise, cracked, and crevassed, and huge. As we watched, big chunks of ice periodically cracked off and crashed into the sea. I have never seen anything like it.

Our first stop after the Hubbard Glacier was Juneau, third largest city in Alaska, and unreachable by car. After traveling on our charter bus through Juneau's suburb, and past schools, we suddenly found ourselves at the end of the Mendenhall Glacier. This was very cool, and very weird. I mean - can you imagine having this massive glacier at the end of your surburb - just a mile or two past your neighborhood school?

I did a quick walk to a humongous waterfall at the end of the glacier, stood in the spray of it, arms wide - and just let my body soak in the magnificence of the glacier. When I returned to the bus I found that Scott had found one of my dad's maps at the Visitor's Center and bought it. The thought that my dad's map had found its way to the Mendenhall Glacier Visitor's Center put a grin on my face. I love those kinds of connections.

Then it was back on the cruise ship - next stop: the historical old mining town of Skagway. Skagway really appealed to the history-lover in me, and I loved the people I met there. At Skagway's National Historical Park, I met a National Park guide named Ruth Kerr who also works in the Klondike Gold Rush National Historical Park in Seattle, at the other end of the trek to find gold in the Klondike. As Ruth said, "It takes 1500 miles to tell the story."

Skagway was scrappy. We had a snack at the old saloon, wandered past a building with sticks for siding, and another building that showed the Russian influence in Alaska with a really cool gold-colored dome.

After our tour of the town we took a bus up to the White Pass summit, where we saw a couple of snowboarders who'd spent a happy day climbing to the top of snow patches and boarding down them. I went up to talk to them and discovered that they had friends who lived, like, three miles from our home, back in Bow, Washington! What are the odds of meeting people in the hinterlands of Alaska with connections to Bow?! Connections, baby. I love these connections.

When we boarded back onto the ship we "set sail" for the old Tlingit fishing village of Hoonah, in Icy Cove, to embark on a whale-watching tour. There is no guarantee, of course, that one will see whales on a whale-watching tour - but we did see several whales rising out of the water, and a couple of orcas, too.

Next we dropped anchor in Ketchikan. I absolutely loved Ketchikan! It rains 13 feet a year in Ketchikan – it's the rainiest city in Alaska – but I told everyone I've always been really lucky with the weather – and, sure enough, we were blest with a sparkly, sunshiny day while we were there. After a couple hours wandering Ketchikan, we took a tour bus to Saxman Village, a town established by natives from the Tlingit tribe at the turn of the last century. Members of the tribe performed a couple of traditional Tlingit dances for us and then welcomed those of us from the "outside" to come up and join them in a final dance. A nice lady from the Raven clan wrapped a Tlingit shawl around my shoulders and told me to bend my knees and bob to the left and bob to the right to the beat of the drums - and I was good to go!

After the dancing, we had the great privilege of visiting the totem-carving workroom, filled with the scent of fresh cedar, and being introduced to Nathan Jackson, a member of the Tlingit tribe and a world-renowned artist/totem carver.

Back in Ketchikan for a couple hours, we took the walk along the Creek Street boardwalk. If you ever find yourself in Ketchikan, I highly recommend you check out the boardwalk - the former Red Light district of the old mining and fishing town. The boardwalk is lined with historical old stores featuring art by local artists, and follows a creek that, at this time of the year, is filled with salmon making their way to their spawning waters.

While we were there, we watched a harbor seal circling around in the creek, looking for lunch - and when he finally was ready to catch a fish, that seal moved like a missile through the water - he was unbelievably fast and dexterous - turning abruptly, racing one direction and then the other. The salmon did not have much of a chance against his speedy attack.

I enjoyed our time in Ketchikan very much - it reminded me a lot of the Puget Sound - totem pole village, glaciers, snow-topped mountains – only everything seemed way bigger somehow – bigger totem poles, bigger glaciers, bigger mountains.

At the end of the day we boarded our ship one final time. The next day would be spent traveling through the Inside Passage to Vancouver, BC.

Meanwhile, back on the ship…

I haven't talked about what was actually going on IN the cruise ship whilst we were on it, have I? Well, let's see... somewhere people were gambling – but none of them were us (why *any*one would go on an Alaskan cruise to spend time inside gambling is a mystery to me) - some-other-where people were dancing, there were some shows – we all went to a variety show together one night which was pretty fun – there were lounges with music, there was tons of food (literally – tons of food), and we had a couple of really great waiters, Sahan and Reuben, serving us at our assigned dining room table. Of course, the best thing about the cruise was the chance to spend time with Bev, Matt, Jordan, and Marilyn – we had never before had the opportunity to spend time together like this – and they are really wonderful people to spend time *with* – funny, generous, smart, and kind.

And there was one thing I was really hoping to do on the cruise ship before we debarked for good – I wanted to dance one time with Scott. Our last night on board the cruise ship, Scott and I made a pact to dance together – if we could find the right song. But, as we traveled from lounge to lounge, none of the music seemed quite right for us. We had just about given up – were, in fact, ready to call it a night – when suddenly… whoah. Scott had once told me that the song that he most attached to me, in his mind, was "My Girl" by the Temptations. And there it was! We both looked at each other, our eyebrows raised – I think my jaw dropped – and then we were, finally, dancing together. It had been a really long time since we'd danced together, and I enjoyed it very much.

The Inside Passage is beautiful - dotted with small forested islands, and rocky coves and with craggly, snow-capped mountains seeming to rise right out of the sea. The day was sunny and the waters sparkled and it was a perfect day to be on a cruise ship.

When we docked in Vancouver, I felt like I was home. Bellingham is just a short hop across the border from Vancouver, and it has the same feel to it - both cities are teeming with active, outdoorsy folks -

paddle-boarders, kayakers, bicyclers - and both cities feature artists and street performers, and they both have great public markets for buying fresh produce and local art.

While I was wandering through Vancouver's Public Market, I saw these two chaps sitting on stools at a bar facing out into the crowd, munching chocolaty baked goods, and people-watching. I could tell they were enjoying the people who passed by, as much as the pastries in their hands. These were my kind of folks. I went up and introduced myself to them and chatted with them for a bit. Although Sean was originally from Vancouver, he currently lives in Brazil and had returned to Vancouver for a vacation to visit his friend, Kevin. (Sean highly recommended the chocolate mousse from Stuart's Baked Goods.)

We'd been told by our trip's Go-Ahead tour guide, Bob (a more calm and patient soul I have never met - he is a former FBI agent, and a whole book could probably be written just on his life) that a limo would take us to the airport the next day. Having experienced a "limo" ride from an airport before, what I was expecting was more of a van. But an actual stretch limousine showed up at our hotel door to take us to the airport! And so, joined by three of our fellow tourists, Barb, Frances, and Kelly, my husband and I ended our epic adventure to Alaska and back with a luxury limo ride!

Our journey to Alaska and back had started at the Seattle-Tacoma Airport, and took us to Anchorage, Denali National Park, Juneau, Skagway, Ketchikan, and Vancouver, BC. - a blur of mountains, glaciers, wildlife, totem poles, human life, history, color, sweets, music, dancing, laughter, and breath-taking beauty.

I shall be forever grateful to Matt and Bev for sharing their Alaskan adventure with us at a time when it didn't look, from a "realistic" and limited standpoint, like that kind of adventure would be in any way possible for us.

Proof, once again, that nothing can stop the flow of Good in our lives.

The Adventuress

Life, he was fond of telling himself,
was like an ocean. You can either grind your
way across it like a motorboat or you can
follow the winds and the currents— in other
words, go sailing.
– Douglas Adams

...I always feel that prayer is a silent
thing, an opening of the heart. To ask for
earthly benefits, to reel out a list of
requirements and expect them to be supplied
is not prayer. It is putting God in the same
category as an intelligent grocer.
- D.E. Stevenson

Desire is prayer; and no loss can
occur from trusting God with our desires,
that they may be moulded and exalted before
they take form in words and in deeds.
- Mary Baker Eddy, *Science and*
Health with Key to the Scriptures

...with God all things are possible.
- Matthew 19: 26

For a couple of years I'd watched the tall ships come into Bellingham Bay and dreamed of one day sailing on one. There was just something about the majesty of them at full sail – something intrepid and brave and dauntless that called to me. Probably I'd read *Captain Blood* one too many times.

I never imagined I'd ever actually find myself sailing on a tall ship. But, then again, I also never closed the door on the possibility. If there's one thing I've learned in the last several years, it's that no good thing is impossible to Life.

I've also learned that you can't try to outline these things – it's pointless to try to confine good into some human plan of how, where, and when. When it comes – and good *will* come – all you need to be is ready and willing to receive it.

When the opportunity to sail on a tall ship arrived, it arrived quite suddenly, and from a completely unexpected quarter.

At the beginning of my second year at the alternative high school our new science and environmental education teacher, Bev, asked the rest of the staff if any of us would be willing to give up an afternoon of the coming weekend to become acquainted with the *Sound Experience* marine education program. The *Sound Experience* program is conducted on board a tall ship named *The Adventuress.* Was I willing to give up a Saturday afternoon to take a free ride aboard The *Adventuress*?

I thought about it… not at all… and immediately said yes.

It was a perfect October afternoon when we arrived at Seattle's Elliot Bay Marina for our sail aboard *The Adventuress* - the sun was shining, the reds and golds in the trees were reflected in a beautiful array in the bay, and the air was filled with the tangy smell of the saltwater and the calls of seagulls. It was one of those days when there was no sense of rush or hurry or panic - one of those days when I felt safe to open my heart wide to whatever was coming my way. I knew, instinctively, that this day was a precious gift, and I was going to enjoy and appreciate every lovely moment of it.

It was not hard to find the tall ship amongst the other boats in the marina – there were no other boats for which it could possibly be mistaken. As I looked at it, I realized that it was probably the very ship I'd seen in Bellingham Bay now and then (and the crew later confirmed this for me). The tall ship was celebrating the centennial anniversary of its launching. It was a magnificent old schooner of polished wood and brass, and with crisp white gaff-rigged sails that snapped in the breeze. There were two berths – one for females and one for gents; a tiny little latrine, or head, complete with shower; a built-in aquarium for studying plankton and other sea life; and a galley with the smell of freshly-baked chocolate chip cookies wafting from it. We were treated like royalty by the crew. Well, working royalty. Actually, one of the best parts of the cruise on the tall ship was being given the opportunity to work on her. Those of us who were visiting for the afternoon were considered crew, too – we hoisted and lowered the sails, sang sea shanties, and kept an eye out for interesting sea creatures to study.

The sail was fantastic! – just as I imagined it would be! The company was congenial, the weather perfect, and the lessons we learned about history and marine biology were interesting and fun. We couldn't have asked for a more perfect day for our sail - sunny skies, and a good wind to keep the sails full.

And... whoah... this just occurred to me: If I hadn't left my other job – the one that paid well, but no longer suited me – and taken the job teaching for less money at the non-profit, I wouldn't have had this opportunity to sail on *The Adventuress*. Supply does not always come in the form of money. I wouldn't have traded my chance to ride on *The Adventuress* for any amount of money.

Just Who Do You Think You Are?!

He attacked everything in life with a mixture of extraordinary genius and naive incompetence and it was often difficult to tell which was which.
- Douglas Adams

"Whatever you do, do it well," said Markie. "If you respect yourself you will be too proud to do it badly."
- D.E. Stevenson

Today you are You, that is truer than true. There is no one alive who is Youer than You.
- Dr. Seuss

In the textbook for Christian Science, *Science and Health with Key to the Scriptures*, Mary Baker Eddy points out that "Jesus'system of healing received no aid nor approval from other sanitary or religious systems, from doctrines of physics or of divinity…" Did this lack of approval stop Jesus from fulfilling his mission, from healing, and accomplishing what he was sent here to accomplish? Did he wait around for permission to heal and do his life's work? Nope, He had the approval of God, Love, and that's the only approval that concerned him.

Okay, listen, if you want to paint your neighbor's house or rearrange his furniture or drive his car to work – it might be a good thing to wait for his approval before doing these things. His house, furniture, and car do not belong to you, and it is not your business to take it upon yourself to paint, rearrange, or drive what doesn't belong to you, without permission.

However, if you are waiting for someone else's approval to be who YOU are and to live YOUR life – well, that's just silly. We who live in the U.S. of A. live in a time of wonderful freedom and incredible invention, and it behooves us to take advantage of this. If you want to move or travel – you don't need to wait for the government's approval. Just do it. If you want to leave your job, or switch schools, or switch majors – that is your choice, not anyone else's. You need no one else's approval to attend the church of your choice, or to choose not to attend a church at all. If consenting adults of whatever gender, sexual orientation, race, or religion choose to build a life together – they don't need anyone else's permission or approval. And we live at a time when we no longer have to wait for someone else to decide if our writing is book-worthy or our voice is worth recording – the technology to put our words and voices out there is available to anyone with access to a computer – and no one else's approval is necessary.

You need not wait for approval, my friend
You need not wait to practice zen
You need not wait to sing and soar
You need not wait – not one second more!
You need no one's permission to be who you are,
to express and reflect and travel far.
If you want to write and publish a book
or cook up the recipes of a cordon bleu cook
If you want to dance or hop or run

don't wait for permission – just get
'er done.
You don't need permission to love
one another –
to be a partner, or friend, or sister or
brother.
No, you need no approval to your
life live.
You were MADE to express your
you-ness,
and your talents to give.

Four years before I left my career in
public education I became friends, over the
internet, with an artist named Kathi who
lived in Nova Scotia, Canada. I wanted to
share my part of the world with Kathi, and,
because she was an artist, I wanted to share
my world in a way worthy of an artist. I
began taking photos to share with her, and I
tried to make them more than just snapshots.
I wanted to create photos that would help
her feel what I was feeling when I was in the
mountains and forests, and looking at the
birds and bay. I experimented with color and
contrast, lighting and reflection and

silhouettes, and looked for the unusual and beautiful all around me.

I started getting positive feedback.

I wondered if maybe I could turn my photos into notecards and sell them somewhere. I asked my friends for advice on what I might need to make notecards and bought cardstock and double-sided tape and – la piece de resistance – a stamp that said "Karen Molenaar Terrell, Photographer" with an email address where people might contact Karen Molenaar Terrell, the photographer.

And then came the business cards. I printed them out from my own computer with the words "Karen Molenaar Terrell, Author and Photographer" lasered on them. Getting the business cards was huge for me. Holding the first one in my hand sort of changed the way I saw myself.

I was very faithful about handing out those business cards the first couple months. I think they were like a crutch at first - sort of holding me up as I found my footing – but after a while I gradually lost interest in them. I didn't need them anymore. They'd served their purpose.

I started three blogs – one of them to share things that make me laugh, one of them for inspirational-metaphysical stuff, and one of them devoted to my photography. And my friend, Kathi, suggested I put my photos on a website called Fine Art America – where people could buy them if they wanted.

And just who did I think I was?! Who did I think I was to call myself a photographer?! Or a writer?! Or an artist?! On the other hand, who was I not to call myself all those things? Why *not* me?

And once again, as I sent my hopes and dreams out into the cosmos, and opened my thought up to all the possibilities of Life, Good happened. One day I got an email from an English professor who was the Editor-in-Chief for the local university's annual *Review*. She wrote: "I'm writing to ask if you might be interested in publishing some of your black-and-white photography in the spring 2014 edition of *Bellingham Review*. I was looking at your work on Fine Art America, and your art so wonderfully captures the spirit of Bellingham and the surrounding area."

I know! Way cool, right? I never could have seen that one coming. And I love that! Life is just full of wonderful gifts if you let them happen.

(Ahem. I said yes.)

Encouragement from people like the professor at the local university has been hugely helpful for me. It's impelled me to want to go up to the next level with my work. In II *Timothy* 2, we read, "Study to shew thyself approved unto God, a workman that needeth not to be ashamed…"

It took a certain amount of innocent chutzpah to launch myself into the world as an "author and photographer" - and I'm really glad I did it. Who was I *not* to use the gifts given to me by Life?

And who are you not to use *your* gifts?

"I told them a story my dad used to tell me… He always used to tell me… 'Russ, why not you? Why can't you be a world champion or whatever else you want to be?'… I had a lot of critics tell me, 'He's too short…' and I wasn't going to believe it.

I wasn't going to allow that to stop me from doing what God put me on this earth for."
— Russell Wilson, Seahawks quarterback

The talents He gives we must improve.
Mary Baker Eddy

"God, Please Help Karen Get Her Shit Together"

She did not allow her sense of humor to interfere with business; she only used it as a sauce to make the boiled fish more interesting - so to speak.
- D.E. Stevenson

People don't come to church for preachments, of course, but to daydream about God.
- Kurt Vonnegut

I love deadlines. I like the whooshing sound they make as they fly by.
- Douglas Adams

Last year I served another term as first reader at the local Christian Science church. For those of you who aren't familiar with Christian Science church services, the first reader puts together the readings and conducts the mid-week testimony meetings, and, together with the second reader, presents the weekly lesson-sermon on Sundays. I have been both a first reader and a second reader in the past, so I was not ignorant of the sizable commitment I was making when I agreed to serve as first reader last year, but I wanted to do this for my church. We were going through a transition from "the old" to "the new" and I wanted to help us get there.

Although the readership is a humongous commitment, in some ways it's also the easiest role in the church, and the most fun. The first reader gets to pick out the hymns and the Wednesday night topics – and, of course, when I am first reader I pick out stuff that *I* want to sing, and read about. When I'm first reader there's no one trying to boss me around, or trying to herd me to an usher meeting, Reading Room meeting, or Sunday School meeting, and no team of people with whom I need to figure out schedules. As a reader, I know exactly where I'm supposed to be, when I'm supposed to be there, and what I'm supposed to be doing. I very much like that part of being a reader.

And I could not have asked to have a better partner on the podium. Liz served as second reader last year, and she is a joy –

fun, smart, great sense of humor – and she's a really classy dresser, too (which sort of balances out my own "dang!-what-do-I-have-to-wear-that's-clean?" look).

Most Sundays Liz beat me to church, and had already put the hymn numbers up for me, had her second reader stuff laid out on the podium, and was looking classy and put-together when I came bursting through the door. But there was one Sunday when I actually beat her by about ten minutes! I was feeling pretty smug about it, too. "Liz! I got here before you this morning! Aren't you proud of me?"

"Yes," Liz said, "I'm very proud of you. Every day I pray, 'God, please help Karen get her shit together this week' and I'm so glad to see my prayers worked."

Ohmygosh. The laughter just burst from me – I was laughing so hard I bent up double and had to wipe the tears from my face. I had a hard time keeping a straight face during the service that day. I still get a grin on my face when I think about Liz's response to me.

Liz is exactly the kind of person I'd like to see reading from every Christian Science podium.

The Unitarian Universalist Service

So, my argument is that as we become more and more scientifically literate, it's worth remembering that the fictions with which we previously populated our world may have some function that it's worth trying to understand and preserve the essential components of, rather than throwing out the baby with the bath water; enable us to work and live together. Therefore, I would argue that though there isn't an actual God, there is an artificial God, and we should probably bear that in mind.
- Douglas Adams

In order not to seem a spiritual quadriplegic to strangers trying to get a fix on me, I sometimes say I'm a Unitarian Universalist. So that denomination claims me as one of their own.
- Kurt Vonnegut

The vital part, the heart and soul of Christian Science, is Love.
- Mary Baker Eddy

There's this quiz you can take on the internet that tells you to what religion your beliefs most correspond. Whenever I'd take this quiz – the Belief-o-Matic quiz – I'd get labeled 100% Unitarian Universalist (while with the religion I was raised in, Christian Science, I'd range anywhere from 33% to 65%, depending on the day). The results of this quiz made me kind of curious about the U-U church. Seeing as how I was supposed to be one of them, philosophically, I figured the Unitarian Universalists must be really splendid people, right?

And sometimes, when I was feeling particularly inspired by life, and wanting to share my inspiration with others (or feeling particularly preachy, and wanting to sermonize), I'd kind of roll around the idea – in a not-really-serious way - of someday becoming a U-U minister and having the opportunity to share my great wisdom and stuff from a pulpit. And maybe getting paid for it. That would be kind of cool, I thought.

A couple years after I first took the Belief-o-Matic quiz and started having my not-very-serious daydreams about becoming a preacher-woman, I ran into the parent of one of my former students at a musical song-singing get-together. I no longer remember how I ended up there or who invited me – but I do remember how happy I was to see Sally again. One thing led to another and a couple days later I sent her a copy of my book, *Blessings: Adventures of a Madcap Christian Scientist*. After she read it, she asked me if I'd ever be interested in sharing my way of life as a Christian Scientist with her Unitarian Universalist congregation, and I said sure – I could do that.

Time went by, and I sort of forgot all about it...

In January or February one of my Facebook friends asked me to list 20 albums that were meaningful to me in some way. It took me a few days to think about this. I listed the usual stuff from my generation - Grateful Dead's *Truckin'*, stuff by the Traveling Wilburys, Chicago, Simon and Garfunkle. Then I realized there were a couple albums that were meaningful to me because of the cozy memories they brought back from my childhood – albums my mom and dad used to play on their big reel-to-reel audiotape machine: *Scheherazade*, Marty Robbins' *50 Guitars Go South of the Border*, the *Lawrence of Arabia* theme song. I hadn't heard any of that music for more than 30 years, but just thinking about those albums brought back sentimental feelings. I especially tried to remember what *Scheherazade* sounded like.

Not long after the FB question about music, Sally emailed me out of the blue and asked me if I could speak at her U-U church in a few weeks. She told me her church would pay me to do this. (!) I said yes.

Okay, now that I was *actually* going to be speaking in front of the U-U congregation – and not just having a not-very-serious fantasy about it - I have to admit I was a little nervous about the whole adventure. Although, as a teacher, I was used to speaking in front of teenagers, I was not so used to speaking in front of grown-ups, and certainly not about my beliefs.

I solicited advice from some of my friends.

David Allen, whose great wisdom is featured in *The Madcap Christian Scientist's Middle Book*, messaged me this sage advice: "Make sure to shamelessly plug all your books. From what I've seen on TV interviews, this should take up 80% of your allotted time. Allow time for Q-and-A, but as soon as an uncomfortable question comes up, change the subject, and use that opportunity to plug a different book. Alternatively, you can abruptly end the talk by 'remembering' that you have an interview by the Pulitzer Prize committee to get to."

As always, I found David's suggestions very helpful.

The week before my talk, as a sort of preparation, I attended a U-U service for the first time. Everyone was very welcoming, and I felt right at home. Several of the congregants mentioned that they were looking forward to seeing me again the next week, and hearing what I had to say about Christian Science.

How, I wondered, could I share my understanding of Christian Science in 45 minutes, without either boring everyone or looking like a complete nut? Yikes, right?

And then it came to me – Love! Love is where I needed to start. Love is where I needed to end, too. Love is, for me, the essence of Christian Science – the essence, really, of anything and everything that matters. Now I had my topic. Sally asked me to share what a typical service might be like in a Christian Science church, and that gave me a format. I decided to offer a sort of abbreviated amalgamation of a Wednesday night testimony meeting and a Sunday church service – and picked readings from the *Bible* and the Christian Science textbook that went with the topic of Love.

The offering came before I went up to the podium to speak, and as I was sitting there, listening to Sally play the offertory, it hit me all of a sudden that I recognized that music! Was it…? Could it be…??! I looked over at the program Scott was holding to see what was listed as the offertory – and saw that Sally was, indeed, playing *Scheherazade*!! Whoah, right?! How cool is

THAT?! (Later Sally told me that she'd never heard that song until a few months before when she'd picked it up at a music store. I love when stuff like that happens!)

And then it was my turn to speak.

I explained that I was not an official spokesperson for the Christian Science church, and was in no way representative of all Christian Scientists - that I could only share my own experience with this way of life, and my own understanding of Christian Science. I talked for a moment, too, about the Christian Science concept of "God" as Love - not an anthropomorphic being zapping his children to hell with lightning bolts. I shared the synonyms the discoverer of Christian Science, Mary Baker Eddy, gives for God: Principle, Mind, Soul, Spirit, Life, Truth, and Love. I asked the congregation to substitute the word "Love" or the word "Truth" for God whenever I read the word "God" from the *Scriptures* or the Christian Science textbook. And I asked the congregation to join with me in using the service to send out thoughts of peace and love into the world consciousness. I told them we were going to heal the world. My

new friends smiled. Unitarian Universalists
are good sports.

I read a quote by Nando Parrado
from the book *Miracle in the Andes: 72
Days in the Mountains and My Long Trek
Home*, which I think expresses really well
my own thoughts about God. "I did not feel
God as most people see Him. I did feel
something larger than myself, something in
the mountains and the glaciers and the
glowing sky that, in rare moments, reassured
me, and made me feel that the world was
orderly and loving and good... It was simply
a silence, a wholeness, an awe-inspiring
simplicity. It seemed to reach me though my
own feelings of love, and I have often
thought that when we feel what we call love,
we are really feeling our connection to this
awesome presence... It wasn't cleverness or
courage or any kind of competence or savvy
that saved us, it was nothing more than love,
our love for each other, for our families, for
the lives we wanted so desperately to live."

Then I read the passages I'd picked
out from the *Bible* and *Science and
Health;* read the words to Mary Baker
Eddy's poem, *Love;* played *In His Eyes* by

74

Mindy Jostyn on the CD-player; and, at the end, invited the congregation to join me in a rousing rendition of "We Shall Overcome." And they did!!!

There was power in that room. A flood of hope, joy, love, and courage was sent out into the universal consciousness by my new friends at the U-U church.

Did you feel it?

Thou to whose power our hope we give,
Free us from human strife.
Fed by Thy love divine we live,
For Love alone is Life;
And life most sweet as heart to heart
Speaks kindly when we meet and part.

- from the poem *Love* by Mary Baker Eddy

Humoristianity

On August 20, 2007, Karen says:
I've decided to create a new religion.
People belonging to this religion will call
themselves "Humoristians." Here are the 5
tenets:

1) You must be able to laugh at
yourself.

2) You must be able to recognize
how ludicrous your beliefs might appear to
others.

3) You must want nothing but good
for everyone, everywhere in the universe.

4) You must have a natural aversion
to meetings, committees, and scheduled
events (as we will be having none of those).

5) You must enjoy the humor of Jon
Stewart, Steven Colbert, Tom Lehrer, and
Jerry Seinfeld (if you're a Jerry Lewis kind
of guy, you might want to think about
starting your own religion - although we
wish you nothing but good).

So, have I told you about the time I
started my own religion? After I'd been on
the Amazon religion discussion forum for a

month or so I woke up one morning with the voice of God (or something) in my head, telling me it was time to, yea and verily, start my own religion and stuff. I had not been on the forum long, but I had been on long enough to realize that the one thing that seemed to be desperately needed was the opportunity to laugh at ourselves. It seemed to me that some people were taking themselves and their beliefs waaay too seriously.

I started a thread called "Humoristians" and was soon joined by some of my favorite characters on the forum – atheists and agnostics, a pantheist, several Buddhists, a Lutheran, a Methodist or two, a self-avowed sophist, a couple of people with Mormon roots, a Discordian, and a host of other personalities from a wide array of beliefs, backgrounds, and geographic locations.

And ohmygosh, it was fun!

Our fledgling little church grew rapidly and reached people around the globe. One of the highlights, for me, was when we heard from a soldier in Afghanistan who told us she'd found our thread when she was recovering from an illness and our nonsensical little dialogue totally cheered her up.

Eventually we all drifted off the forum and the Humoristian temple there closed its doors. But we met up again with each other on Facebook, and Humoristianity continues to live - although in a different form. (The founding and history of the Humoristian church can be found in our book, *The Humoristian Chronicles*.)

I have a difficult time relating to people who can't laugh at themselves, or let me laugh at myself. And I have a difficult time relating to people who feel the need to "correct" my thought, manage me, fix me, or "pray" for me without being asked by me to do so.

I have found that sermonizing bossy britches busybodies can be found amongst pretty much every group of people – both religious and non-religious. I tend to avoid sermonizing bossy britches busybodies – even the Christian Scientist ones. Maybe especially the Christian Scientist ones. This may sound weird, but I really have very

little in common with those Christian
Scientists who can't occasionally laugh at
themselves and their circumstances. We may
all believe that God is "Principle, Mind,
Soul, Spirit, Life, Truth, and Love" (the
synonyms given by Mary Baker Eddy in the
Christian Science textbook), and we may all
believe that God heals, but if a Christian
Scientist can't laugh at herself then her
approach to life and its challenges is going
to be very different from mine. I believe I
actually have more in common with, say, an
atheist Humoristian than I do with a
Christian Scientist non-Humoristian

Just as Bossybritches Busybodies
can be found in pretty much every group of
people, Humoristians can, too. I count
amongst my friends Jewish Humoristians,
atheist Humoristians, Christian Scientist
Humoristians, and Buddhist, Catholic, and
Methodist Humoristians, among others.

There are times when, if I were to be
asked what religion I affiliate myself with, I
think I might actually be inclined to answer
"Humoristianity". A sense of humor about
life, and about themselves, is the one thing
the people I feel a kinship with all have in

common – whether they call themselves atheists, Catholics, Christian Scientists, Buddhists, pantheists, Lutherans, Methodists, or Mormons.

Long live Humoristianity! Long may we don her Groucho glasses and play her kazoos!

People are so funny, aren't they? I mean they're so interesting - and all different. They're all so busy living their own lives (if you know what I mean), and they're all so certain that they're frightfully important. And the queer thing is that the very busy, serious ones are much the funniest.
- D.E. Stevenson

Laughs are exactly as honorable as tears. Laughter and tears are both responses to frustration and exhaustion, to the futility of thinking and striving anymore. I myself prefer to laugh, since there is less cleaning up to do afterward - and since I can start thinking and striving again that much sooner.
- Kurt Vonnegut

Finding My Tribe

*So then, a few years ago, I was
introduced to someone who became a great
friend of mine, Michael Nesmith, who has
done a number of different things in his
career: In addition to being a film producer,
he was originally one of the Monkees. Which
is kind of odd when you get to know him,
because he's such a serious, thoughtful,
quiet chap, but with quiet reserves of impish
glee...I just hope that there will be other
projects in the future that he and I will work
on together, because I like him enormously
and we got on very well together.*
- Douglas Adams

*In a new friend we start life anew,
for we create a new edition of ourselves and
so become, for the time being, a new
creature. Barbara had never done this
interesting thing before. She had lived all
her life in Silverstream and her neighbors
were people who had known her from
childhood, and therefore had a preconceived
idea of her, so engrained, that they never
saw her at all, any more than they saw the*

sponge which accompanied them daily into their baths. In creating a new Barbara for Jerry Cobbe, Barbara created a new facet of herself and was enlarged by it.
- D.E. Stevenson

Human beings prefer to organize in tribes, into groups of people who share a leader or a culture or a definition of normal. And the digital revolution has enabled and amplified these tribes, leaving us with millions of silos, groups of people who respect and admire and support choices that outsiders happily consider weird, but that those of us in the tribe realize are normal (our normal)... The ability to reach and change those around you has been changed forever by the connections of the Internet and the fact that anyone, anywhere can publish to the world... the Internet connects and protects the weird by connecting and amplifying their tribes.
- Seth Godin

When I wrote my first book, *Blessings: Adventures of a Madcap Christian Scientist*, and even, I guess, when

I wrote *The Madcap Christian Scientist's Middle Book*, I never would have imagined that there would come a time when I would actually be visited by people from Minnesota, New York, Michigan, and Texas whom I had met on a discussion board. I mean... how *could* I have imagined that? When I wrote my first book I didn't even know these people existed, yet – had never, in fact, been on an Internet discussion board in my life – and had only recently bought my first little laptop.

The Internet has opened up a whole 'nother world for us, hasn't it?

And it has helped me find my tribe.

I know this is going to come as a shock to many of you – but... ahem... I am kind of an odd duck. I'm a Christian Scientist, but I'm not very religious; I enjoy meeting new people, but after 20 minutes of sustained conversation I am exhausted; and, as my son once correctly surmised, I like being liked but I am not willing to change who I am to be liked. To sum it up: I am weird. It's sometimes been hard for me to find other odd ducks like myself in my local community. There have been times when

I've felt really alone, I guess. But the Internet has helped connect me to other folks like myself beyond the boundaries of my part of the world, and I've been very grateful for that.

In the *Madcap Christian Scientist's Middle Book* I talked about a weekend excursion my family and I took to Nova Scotia in 2009 to meet Kathi and Jamie, a couple I'd met through the Humoristian thread on the Amazon discussion forum. (Jamie had come on soon after my opening post and had the good sense to suggest I add Groucho Marx and Monty Python to my list of favorite comedians – he later became the Grand Inquisitor of our one true fallacious faith, and bestowed upon me the title of "Popellina".) That was great fun. And our visit with Kathi and Jamie turned out to be just the beginning of my connecting with others from my "tribe".

Several summers later I met up with New Yorkers Sandy (another Humoristian friend I'd met on Amazon's discussion forum) and her husband, Danny. They were passing through Seattle on a trip and I drove down and spent some time with them at the Pike Place Market in Seattle. They were both smart and funny, and shared my political views, and Danny and I shared teacher stories with each other.

Not long after my visit with Sandy and Danny, another founding member of the Humoristian faith, my friend from Michigan, David "Runny Babbit" Allen, Patron Saint of Talking Animals, and his wife, Sue, and two wonderful daughters stopped by our house for a couple days on their vacation along the west coast. David had been one of the first people to join me on the Humoristian thread and was my second official friend on the Amazon forum. David brought me a flute he had made out of Michigan sassafrass and a Petoskey stone and played native American flute music on it for me. David and Sue and the girls also joined us for a hike up Sauk Mountain – and I was so very proud of Sue and the youngest Allen daughter, who both suffer from a pronounced fear of heights, for negotiating those Sauk Mountain switchbacks step-by-step and persevering until they made it to the top. Along the way we saw wildflowers –

red Indian paintbrush and wild phlox – and a friendly little marmot, who poked his head over a boulder and watched us all with keen fascination and a twitching nose.

It was hard to say good-bye to the Allen family. (I'm hoping someday we'll be able to visit them in their home state – maybe I'll be able to write about that in my next book.)

The following summer my Humoristian Texan friend, Heather, who was my first official friend on the Amazon forums, contacted me to let me know she would be in Oregon for a few days – and would I be able to meet her somewhere to spend an afternoon together? - we decided to meet half-way between where she was in Oregon and where I live in northern Washington and spent an afternoon together in Olympia, Washington – one of my favorite little towns in the world – a university town with an alternative culture, sitting on the southern tip of the Puget Sound. We ate lunch at an Italian Restaurant there and then spent a couple hours exploring the Olympia Farmers' Market. It was so fun to finally meet Heather in the person, and to actually be able to reach over and give her a hug.

And just two months ago my Humoristian friend, Marissa, let me know that she was taking a business trip to Vancouver, BC, just an hour to the north of me. How could we NOT meet, right?!! Marissa booked passage on the AmTrak train from Vancouver to Bellingham and I picked her up at the train station. I was really nervous and excited to meet Marissa. She'd always been one of my most favorite posters on the Amazon forum – witty, thoughtful, not afraid to challenge nonsense, and not afraid to laugh at herself, either. In the last couple of years Marissa has had to make choices that took a great deal of courage to make and I hope that someday she'll share her story with the world. For now, suffice it to say, I have a lot of respect for who she is.

Marissa and I went out to eat – Italian, again – what can I say? I love Italian. Marissa spent the night at my house - my husband snapped a photo of the two of us in our fairy wings and Groucho glasses (now THERE's a fashion statement) – and then I took her to the bus station early the next morning and – poof! – she was gone. Too short. Too little time. But I'm hoping there will be a next time that is longer.

Several years ago I received a message through another Christian Scientist from a man in Florida named Chip who had just finished reading my book, *Blessings: Adventures of a Madcap Christian Scientist*. Chip wrote, "I was searching high and low on how to find an address or way to find Karen for having the courage to express her own unique identity as Love's reflection, and in doing so, to echo a resounding 'Yes' to my own inner sense of Love's direction in my life."

Chip's kind words meant a lot to me, and I wrote him back right away to thank him. And so began our friendship.

When I first met Chip he had been a registered nurse for 28 years, and had been with his partner for "almost as long." As a medical nurse and a gay man he had "found roadblocks" in feeling closer to the Christian Science community. He said, "…but you know, I just really love to be with folks who are making an effort to be closer to God Who is All Good and All Love!"

Chip's friendship over the last several years has been a wonderful blessing to me. He always seems to know when I most need an encouraging word, a bit of email inspiration, and a cheering picture of flowers or pets or his family.

I have not (yet) met Chip in the person, but I know him. I know his patients are blest to have him in their lives – his kindness and caring come through in every word he writes me. I know his family and friends and partner are blest to have him in THEIR lives, too. And I know I am blest to have him in mine.

Last autumn I joined up with others on Facebook and liked the "Paradoxical Commandments" page. *The Paradoxical Commandments*, written by Dr. Kent M. Keith, are wonderful life-maxims advising us to "do good anyway". They end with this "commandment": "Give the world the best you have and you will get kicked in the teeth. Give the best you have anyway." I love that! Do good anyway – because what's the alternative, right?

Soon I had a friend request from a Rwandan named Norman Kagera. I didn't realize Norman had found me on the Paradoxical Commandments page – I thought he'd maybe found me through my Christian Scientist connections or something – but I happily accepted his friend request. And then, because he said he'd like to read my book, *Blessings: Adventures of a Madcap Christian Scientist*, I mailed it off to Rwanda and waited to hear if it got there. After a couple weeks Norman let me know the book had arrived and he was reading it, and then he sent me this message (I am leaving this quote unedited because I love the African accent I hear in it): "Hi Karen!!after reading your books,now i understand you much better and am convinced that you are a good person,lovable,humorous,a good speaker"that is i would love to hear you speak in person"i mean-i just love you Karen.i now feel like you are an African and i can boast of having a new and a good friend.am excited and happy for you alltogether.thank you for the gift.it is,do i say amiracle or what?ok i say the best early Christmas gift i have ever recieved!!! It like i now know you in person.MY GOOD FRIEND."

Norman's words "i now feel like you are an African" really touched me. I think that may be one of the nicest things anyone has ever said to me. Norman later told me that his son loves my book and carries it with him to school. I cannot tell you how much that news touched my heart.

Norman is part of my tribe now, and I feel part of his.

My life has been so enriched by my new friends. I have found my tribe and they are all over the world.

* I included the Douglas Adams quote about his friend Michael Nesmith because Michael Nesmith identifies himself as a Christian Scientist, and the fact that Adams respected and liked him gives me hope that Adams might not have written me off as a COMPLETE loony.

A Union of Hearts

*Kindred tastes, motives, and aspirations are
necessary to the formation of a happy and
permanent companionship... The scientific
morale of marriage is spiritual unity...
Marriage should signify a union of hearts...
Beholding the world's lack of Christianity
and the powerlessness of vows to make
home happy, the human mind will at length
demand a higher affection. There will ensue
a fermentation over this as over many other
reforms, until we get at last the clear
straining of truth... Matrimony, which was
once a fixed fact among us, must lose its
present slippery footing, and man must find
permanence and peace in a more spiritual
adherence.*
– excerpts from the chapter titled
"Marriage" in *Science and Health with Key
to the Scriptures* by Mary Baker Eddy

*"I know," said Ellen, "I know all
that, John, but I love her just the same."*
- D.E. Stevenson

This year my husband and I celebrated our 30th anniversary. Every year about this time I find myself thinking back to that happy day and the days leading up to it.

You know those shows you see on television where the bride spends HUGE amounts of time, thought, and bucks choosing just the right ring, dress, caterer, flowers, music, photographer, and reception venue for her "big day" – those shows where every minute detail of the wedding production is analyzed, critiqued, and judged for its merits on visual perfection? Where the ceremony is somber and refined and the highlight of the whole shebang is the dress the bride wears?

Yeah. That wasn't us.

My engagement ring was a little garnet ring I picked out from a small jewelry shop in Pike Place Market in Seattle, and the man who sold it to us was cheerfully, flamboyantly, hilariously gay - he had us cracking up the minute we walked into his shop. My wedding dress was the first dress I tried on from the sales rack at our local Bon Marche. Cost me $120. Our minister was a hoot – we'd met with him for a required counseling session, and when he told us that anything he had to say to us would be pretty much useless at this point – because it's really only AFTER the wedding that the bride and groom realize what they've gotten themselves into (we later learned that he'd just recently been divorced), we immediately recognized the man had a sense of humor, and he was, for sure, the minister we wanted officiating our nuptials. The wedding was a joyful, light-hearted affair in a small Methodist church in Gig Harbor – I remember the minister asking us if we really wanted to hold the service in his church – it was very small – could maybe hold 100 people – and very old (it's since been torn down and a larger church built in a different location) – but, for our purposes, that little church was perfect – I liked the cozy smallness of it and the stained glass windows – and from the church's steps we could look out across the water and see Mount Rainier rising above the hills in the distance.

The wedding itself was simple, joyful, and natural. We weren't too concerned with "perfection" – we just wanted our guests to feel comfortable and loved. The reception was held in my parents' backyard – with the sound of laughter, and the smell of daffodils and plum blossoms, filling the air. And we played volleyball in the pasture – the groom's team won, but it was a close game. The minister came to the reception, and fit right in with our hooligan families and friends. Before he left he told us that sometimes he's really worried about the future of the newlyweds he marries – they often seem more concerned about the wedding than the actual marriage - but, after watching us yukking it up with our families and friends, he felt good about being a part of our ceremony. He knew we were going to be alright. We knew how to laugh.

When I think about that day, I can't imagine why anyone would want to deny other people the right to a wedding, and to a life-long commitment in marriage with the partner they love. I can't understand why any heterosexual couple would feel their own marriage is threatened by giving homosexuals the same rights that they have. I feel a real yearning for other folks who love one another, and are brave enough to make a commitment to each other, to be allowed to have what my husband and I were allowed to have.

Happiness is spiritual, born of Truth and Love. It is unselfish; therefore it cannot exist alone, but requires all mankind to share it.
– from the chapter titled "Marriage" in *Science and Health with Key to the Scriptures* by Mary Baker Eddy

The Second Blooming

*I have enjoyed greatly the second
blooming... suddenly you find - at the age of
50, say - that a whole new life has opened
before you.*
- Agatha Christie

*No, she was not like other people.
Other people took grown-up things as a
matter of course - things like late dinner,
and wine, driving cars and going to the
theater; things like marriage and
housekeeping and ordering commodities
from the shops; whereas she was just
playing at it all the time, pretending to be
grown up... she still enjoyed the same things
- ice cream, and sweet cakes , and crumpets
with the butter oozing out of them—and she
still loved being out at night when the stars
were shining, and going late to bed, and
having breakfast in bed. Someday, she was
convinced, somebody would find out that she
was an imposter in the adult world.*
- D.E. Stevenson

Man, governed by immortal Mind, is always beautiful and grand. Each succeeding year unfolds wisdom, beauty, and holiness.
– Mary Baker Eddy

One morning last week I woke up with this incredible feeling of freedom. I woke up feeling young again. When I say I felt "young" again I'm not referring to the pretty young woman I was at, say, twenty-four – the kind of "young" that a lot of women my age seem to want to once again become. No, I'm talking about the kind of young I was at eight, when I twirled around in my alphabet dress on a freshly-mowed lawn, and looked up at a cloudless blue sky, and knew in my wise child's mind that there wasn't any kind of happier than I was at that moment. I woke up feeling like I'd finally made it through to the "other side" – like I'd finally made it to that peaceful place beyond the battlefield – made it through those competitive, ego-filled years of trying to establish a career, find a mate, birth and raise children. I woke up with the feeling that the rivalries that come with youth might at last be behind me, and that I can now allow myself to leave that particular game.

Earlier in the week I'd seen the headline for a story about a celebrity ten years older than me who was going to share her secrets for staying "sultry" at sixty-something. She, apparently, has a boyfriend thirty years younger than her, and, although I didn't read the story – I gathered from the headline that she was going to let all the rest of us "older" women know the secrets of how she'd manage to snag this guy.

I guess I'm glad for this celebrity – glad for her that she's found this new life-partner – but I myself have absolutely no desire or need to learn her secrets for "staying sultry." This doesn't mean that I have no excitement or passion for life, or that I want to shrivel up and cloister myself away or anything – but I'd like to be less "me-centered" than I was in my youth. I'd like to spend less time worrying about wrinkles and gray hair and gaining weight and whether other people think I look good. What I want is… well, what I want is to be able to open my arms up to all the beauty *outside* me, and absorb it into my being, and shine it back out on the world.

I'm glad I was young and pretty once. I look with a certain fondness and affection on pictures of my young self. I was who I needed to be then. But I know it's time to allow my today-self to live. A whole new journey of adventures awaits me, and I'm eager to embark on it.

The great thing about getting older is that you don't lose all the other ages you've been.
- Madeleine L'Engle

As the physical and material, the transient sense of beauty fades, the radiance of Spirit should dawn upon the enraptured sense with bright and imperishable glories.
– Mary Baker Eddy

On Judging Others and Other Really Stupid Stuff I've Done

The members of this Church should daily watch and pray to be delivered from all evil, from prophesying, judging, condemning, counseling, influencing or being influenced erroneously.
- Mary Baker Eddy

Obviously somebody had been appallingly incompetent and he hoped to God it wasn't him.
- Douglas Adams

She was a born meddler. In the garden, for instance, everything was directed by Helen. The raspberry canes, the sweet peas— even the ramblers were obliged to grow in the direction Helen thought best. She bent them to her will, tying them firmly to stake or trellis with pieces of green bass she carried in her pocket for the purpose.
- D.E. Stevenson

*She believed that God liked people in
sailboats much better than He liked people
in motorboats.*
- Kurt Vonnegut

It's occurred to me recently just how much time we spend making judgments on... well, pretty much everything. We have opinions about food, drinks, diets, music, movies, clothing, body shapes, animals, political parties, businesses, groups, religions, ideologies, careers, schooling, people, and we have opinions about *other* peoples' opinions about food, drinks, diets, music, movies, clothing, animals, political parties, businesses, groups, religions, ideologies, careers, schooling, and people. As I've become more conscious of the thoughts that pass through my mind during the course of the day, it's been kind of surprising to see how much of my time is spent making judgments – and I've always considered myself one of the least judgmental people!

Yesterday I found myself thinking about a loved one – about the course of his life – and I found myself wanting him to do this instead of that, to go there instead of here – all well-intentioned wishings, of course, but totally none of my business. And then I found myself doing that thing – that horrible non-Christianly Scientific thing that often tries to pass itself off as "practicing Christian Science" – I found myself trying to "unsee" all the characteristics that my own human opinions had labeled his "faults" – when, really, there's absolutely nothing wrong with what he is right now, and with his life, and with the choices he's making. What's wrong and needs to be corrected is my *own* perception and thoughts and judgments about him.

I used to think I was helping people when I tried to "unsee" what I perceived as a problem for them – if their appearance didn't conform to my opinion of beauty, I tried to help them "fix" it by trying to visualize them in whatever form suited my own opinion of beauty. If a person had what I considered a "bad" personality trait, I tried to "unsee" that personality to make it conform with what I considered a "good" personality. Lord, I am so embarrassed even writing this. I mean... who am *I* to decide what's too thin or too wide, or too weak or too strong? Who am I to decide what specific form someone else's expression of God needs to take? In Christian Science we come to recognize that man and creation are perfect RIGHT NOW – made in the image and likeness of God, as it says in the first chapter of *Genesis*, and as Mary Baker Eddy writes in the Christian Science textbook, *Science and Health with Key to the Scriptures*: "Beauty is a thing of life, which dwells forever in the eternal Mind and reflects the charms of His goodness in expression, form, outline, and color." There is nothing that needs to be fixed, except my own perceptions. Neither I nor anyone else needs to *become* perfect, or develop into something better – we're already there. I like how Edward A. Kimball puts this in *Lectures and Articles on Christian Science*: "We ought to do everything spontaneously, without process or progressive steps. Deny the belief of limitation, obscuration, obstruction, and development. We do not need a long process of development, because all Truth is already developed, and is ours now."

Mary Baker Eddy writes in *Science and Health*: "Human opinions are not spiritual. They come from the hearing of the ear, from corporeality instead of from Principle, and from the mortal instead of from the immortal." Later she writes: "In Christian Science mere opinion is valueless."

Kimball writes: "If the Christian Scientists would be saved they must love. If there is any health in love, in life, you must stop hating. Stop saying hateful things; stop doing hateful things. Simply get to work at number one and make a lover of him as rapidly as possible. Do not think you ought to find fault with someone else; let him alone... 'Don't you think we ought to say something about anybody?' No; there is more abominable cruelty going on about the things you have to say about people than you could put in books. Who is it that sits in judgment on his brother?... Is the cause of Christian Science dear to you? Yes, it is dear enough for you to sit up nights and love, to apply the Golden rule... Let your efforts to get people into the church or your subscriptions go, but do not stop loving." A little later he writes: "Love is the animus, the Principle of Life… Cast out the terrible cruelty that defaces man; lay off the burden that you put upon your brother by reason of condemnation. What a pitiful load we do cast upon man when we enter upon a state of condemnation. How many times do we practice idle criticism, or even mentally lay a burden of reproach and condemnation on our brother, when he forsooth may be in the privacy of thought, weeping hot tears because he is not better able to do his Master's will."

I know, right? There is no way I could put that any better than Kimball does. But I don't need to. What I *do* need to do is follow his advice and simply "get to work at number one…"

Inclusion or Exclusion

"I do not know what the theme of my homily today ought to be. Do I want to talk about the miracle of our Lord's divine transformation? Not really, no. I don't want to talk about His divinity. I'd rather talk about His humanity. I mean, you know, how He lived His life here on earth. His kindness, His tolerance... Listen, here's what I think. I think we can't go 'round measuring our goodness by what we don't do, what we deny ourselves, what we resist, and who we exclude. I think we've got to measure goodness by what we embrace, what we create, and who we include."
– Pere Henri's sermon in *Chocolat*

What you notice depends on who you are.
- Douglas Adams

Trivvie and Ambrose enjoyed the grown-up world in much the same manner as they enjoyed a circus.
- D.E. Stevenson

"It took us that long to realize that a purpose of human life, no matter who is controlling it, is to love whoever is around to be loved."

- Kurt Vonnegut

Chocolat is one of my all-time favorite movies. I love the quirky, lovable characters. I love the images of chocolate being sprinkled, melted, molded, and eaten. I love the movie's wise and wonderful dialogue. I love the setting. I love the... did I mention the chocolate? And I love the movie's message.

If you've never seen the movie, *Chocolat* (or read the book it's based on), let me give a brief summary: A young widow moves into a small French town with her daughter, and opens up a chocolate store. During lent. Yeah. Kind of bad timing. The mayor – a judgmental, and obsessively restrained and rigid fellow, inclined to want to control the behavior of everyone around him – is not pleased by her lack of obedience to the dogma of his church. He proceeds to make life difficult for her –

trying to coerce the people of his town to shun her and her new business.

And this brings me to the gist of what I want to write about in this chapter: exclusivism; elitism; what I call "Country Club Religiousness." In his wonderful sermon, *The Greatest Thing in the World*, Henry Drummond reflects on the Biblical analogy of the sheep being separated from the goats on Judgment Day : "I say the final test of religion at that great Day is not religiousness, but Love; not what I have done, not what I have believed, not what I have achieved, but how I have discharged the common charities of life. Sins of commission in that awful indictment are not even referred to. By what we have not done, by sins of omission, we are judged. It could not be otherwise. For the withholding of love is the negation of the spirit of Christ, the proof that we never knew Him, that for us He lived in vain."

Why do you suppose we sometimes seem to have the need to cast judgment on others? Do you think we feel the need to put others down, shun them, exclude them, and stamp them with labels because we don't realize our *own* wonderfulness? - maybe we feel the need to put others down to somehow feel better about *ourselves*? And do you think that maybe people who join organizations that promote exclusivity are people who have a need to feel like they belong to something "special?" I don't know. I'm not a trained psychologist or anything, and I could just be (once again) full of baloney.

We all know what Jesus said about judging others: "Judge not, that ye be not judged. For with what judgment ye judge, ye shall be judged: and with what measure ye mete, it shall be measured to you again. And why beholdest thou the mote that is in thy brother's eye, but considerest not the beam that is in thine own eye? Or how wilt thou say to thy brother, Let me pull out the mote out of thine eye; and, behold, a beam is in thine own eye? Thou hypocrite, first cast out the beam out of thine own eye; and then shalt thou see clearly to cast out the mote out of thy brother's eye." (Matthew 7)

In the Christian Science textbook, *Science and Health with Key to the Scriptures*, Mary Baker Eddy defines

"Church" as "The structure of Truth and Love; whatever rests upon and proceeds from divine Principle." She writes: "The Church is that institution, which affords proof of its utility and is found elevating the race, rousing the dormant understanding from material beliefs to the apprehension of spiritual ideas and the demonstration of divine Science, thereby casting out devils, or error, and healing the sick."

Note that Eddy doesn't say that the church exists as a place to promote dogma, or to judge others. She doesn't say that the Church exists only for the people who attend service in a material structure, or who obey rules of a human organization. She writes that the purpose of Church is to elevate the "race" – not just some members of the race, but all. She doesn't write that Church exists to serve itself, but that its purpose is to "raise the dormant understanding" of the human race.

Science is inclusive. The laws and rules of physics don't belong just to those who call themselves "physicists": A geologist can't exclude anyone else from studying geology – nobody holds exclusive rights to the study of the earth's surface; The principles of mathematics are universal, and available to everyone who chooses to use them. And, just as geology, physics, and mathematics are inclusive of all mankind, so the Principle of the Christ-Science is universal, and belongs to everyone - nobody has exclusive ownership of Truth; Love, God, doesn't belong to some people, and not others; A human institution doesn't hold exclusive rights to Love's healing power, and can't prevent any of God's children from being one with their Father-Mother, Love.

The healing truths found in Christian Science are available to everyone – not just card-carrying members of the Christian Science church. And what good news that is for humanity!

May our physical housings of Church – our human structures – be perfect manifestations of the "structure of Truth and Love," and may they be filled with a happy fellowship, inclusive of all.

"About astrology and palmistry: they are good because they make people full of possibilities. They are communism at its best. Everybody has a birthday and almost everyone has a palm."
- Kurt Vonnegut

Spinning Heads and Pea Soup

For a moment, nothing happened.
Then, after a second or so, nothing
continued to happen.
- Douglas Adams

Trivvie listened with growing pity to
the stumbling narrative— grown-ups were
odd, she thought (not for the first time).
Here was a perfectly strong and healthy
grown -up with the whole day to do what she
liked with, and nobody to say she mustn't do
this or that or the other, and look at what
she did— it was really pitiable.
- D.E. Stevenson

Evil is nothing, no thing, mind, nor
power. As manifested by mankind it stands
for a lie, nothing claiming to be something,
– for lust, dishonesty, selfishness, envy,
hypocrisy, slander, hate, theft, adultery,
murder, dementia, insanity, inanity, devil,
hell, with all the etceteras that word
includes.
– Mary Baker Eddy

We Bokononists believe that humanity is organized into teams, teams that do God's Will without ever discovering what they are doing. Such a team is called a karass by Bokonon,.. "IF YOU FIND YOUR LIFE tangled up with somebody else's life for no very logical reasons," writes Bokonon, "that person may be a member of your karass."

- Kurt Vonnegut

I've never seen *The Exorcist*, but I have seen that scene with the pea soup and the spinning head – and lately I've seemed to encounter a lot of what I would put in the "pea soup and spinning head" category. There have been times, recently, when personalities have seemed to spin themselves out of alignment with the individuals they really are, spewing out all kinds of hell – anger, frustration, jealousy, fear, revenge, hatred, finger-pointing. And I'm embarrassed to say that on at least a couple occasions recently I myself was the spewer – feeling really angry and hurt that someone who had treated me unfairly while I was in my last year of teaching had managed to get himself promoted to a position of even greater power in the school system.

It none of it felt good.

But then I came across yet another spewing-spinner on a discussion board, and found myself just stepping back and kind of observing in interested fascination as the pea soup flew and the vitriol sprayed. The pea soup and vitriol had been intended for me, but they were so over-the-top and spewed so high in the air that it simply erupted above the spewer's head and ended up landing back on her. It didn't touch me at all. And, standing there on the outside of the mess, it became really clear to me that the spinning-spewing personality was not at all the real individuality of my fellow poster. It was obvious that what I had just witnessed was nothing but a spinning-spewing counterfeit of the real man and woman, made in God's likeness – made in the likeness of Love. And it also became clear to me that I had no desire or need to spend my time engaged in conversation with a counterfeit. I was able to step back and move on and find other interesting dialogues that better served me. I didn't give the counterfeit the power to push me OUT of a space where I belonged, and nor did I give the counterfeit the power to pull me INTO a space where I didn't belong. I didn't have to react or respond to the counterfeit at all.

This encounter with the counterfeit poster helped me come to terms with my feelings of anger and wish for vengeance towards the personality who had treated me so poorly in the past and been promoted. I had to recognize that the real man is the child of God – that God loves him no less than he loves me – and that God is instructing him, and leading him down his own path in life, with its own lessons waiting for him. And none of that is any of my business.

My business is keeping watch on my own thoughts and actions. Mary Baker Eddy writes, "Christian Science commands man to master the propensities, – to hold hatred in abeyance with kindness, to conquer lust with chastity, revenge with charity, and to overcome deceit with honesty. Choke these errors in their early stages, if you would not cherish an army of conspirators against health, happiness, and success."

As Paul says, we all must work out our "own salvation." It's rewarding work. It's satisfying work. And it's also enough work to fill my moments and my days for eternity. Who has time to worry about working out someone ELSE's flaws and foibles, when I have enough of my own to worry about?

Spinning heads and pea soup, be gone!

Clad in the panoply of Love, human hatred cannot reach you. – Mary Baker Eddy

Love has no sense of hatred. – Mary Baker Eddy

Suggestions for Talking with...

Asking people about their opinions is a very good way of making friends. Telling them about your own opinions can also work, but not always quite as well.
– Douglas Adams

She arrived in the middle of a discussion upon international politics. "Look at India," one of the ladies was saying. "Yes, but look at Japan," urged the other with intense vehemence. Barbara was introduced to the ladies, of course, but she never heard their names. They were already labeled, much more legibly in her retentive memory, as Mrs. Japan and Mrs. India.
- D.E. Stevenson

"We're one of the few companies that actually hires men to do pure research. When most other companies brag about their research, they're talking about industrial hack technicians who wear white coats, work out of cookbooks, and dream up an improved windshield wiper for next year's Olds-mobile... Here, and shockingly

few other places in this country, men are paid to increase knowledge, to work toward no end but that   New knowledge is the most valuable commodity on earth. The more truth we have to work with, the richer we become." Had I been a Bokononist then, that statement would have made me howl.

\- Kurt Vonnegut

We should remember that the world is wide; that there are a thousand million different human wills, opinions, ambitions, tastes, and loves; that each person has a different history, constitution, culture, character, from all the rest; that human life is the work, the play, the ceaseless action and reaction upon each other of these different atoms. Then, we should go forth into life with the smallest expectations, but with the largest patience; with a keen relish for and appreciation of everything beautiful, great, and good, but with a temper so genial that the friction of the world shall not wear upon our sensibilities...

\- Mary Baker Eddy (*Miscellaneous Writings)*

I wonder if I might make a few suggestions for conversing with others about religion on a discussion board? As I mentioned in the last chapter, I have had some experience with this, and I'd like to share some of what I've observed and learned.

The most important thing to know, I think, is that if you ever encounter me on a discussion forum I am always, always right. And if you disagree with me about this you are wrong.

Once we have established that basic and most fundamental of all facts, we can move on to other stuff:

- Might I suggest that we never, ever, ever presume to know what other people think, feel, and believe just because they identify themselves as atheist, theist, Christian, Muslim, Jew, Buddhist, pagan, Christian Scientist, or as a member of any other ideology.

- Generalizations, stereotypes, and lumping whole groups of people together as one "type" are not helpful when trying to understand someone else's perspective.
- Don't tell other people what they think. Let them tell you.
- Although pomposity cracks me up, not everyone shares the same reaction as me to puffed-up know-it-allness. Humility is a beautiful thing. Let's be willing to laugh at our own nonsense before we laugh at someone else's.
- Remember that we're all human – we all have our own flaws and foibles – none of us is perfect here. Might I suggest that we correct our own flaws before we start trying to correct someone else's?
- Give each other grace.
- Listen.

More specifically:

When Christians are talking with atheists –

- Do not assume all atheists think, feel, and believe exactly alike – the only thing, really, that all atheists have in common is the conviction that there is no god.
- Do not assume atheists are unfamiliar with religious texts. Some of them are very familiar with religious texts, and, in fact, that is the reason some of them want nothing to do with religion.
- Think about using quotes from the *Bible* sparingly. Remember that not everyone believes the *Bible* in the same way that you do, and quoting from it to prove that you're right probably isn't going to have the effect you're looking for.

- Do not assume that atheists have no sense of ethics, no humanity, or no "moral code" simply because they do not believe in a god. Belief in a god is not necessary to know right from wrong, or to be a kind and compassionate person.
- Do not end disagreements with atheists by condescendingly telling them that you will "pray" for them.

When atheists are talking to theists –

- Do not assume that all theists think, believe, and feel exactly the same about everything.
- Do not assume all theists have the same definition for "God".
- Do not assume every theist is a Christian. There are, among others, theists who are Muslim, Jewish, pagan, and

non-religious. (Contrariwise, not every religious person is theistic – some religions, such as Buddhism and Unitarian Universalism, do not include a belief in a god.)

- Do not assume all theists are superstitious scaredy cats, hoping to God there is an after-life. For some theists a belief in God follows a logical thought process, and doesn't necessarily lead to belief in an after-life.

When atheists are talking to Christians –

- Do not assume all Christians think, feel, and believe exactly the same – the only thing, really, that all Christians have in common is the belief that Jesus was the Christ.

- Do not assume all Christians have the same definition for "God".

- Do not assume all Christians interpret the Scriptures literally.

- Do not assume all Christians belong to the same political party and hold the same political ideology.

- Don't assume that when you're talking with a Christian, you're talking to someone lacking in logic, intelligence, or education. This kind of prejudice tends to lead to a really speedy end of civil discourse.

- Try to quote only sparingly from *The God Delusion* and *God is Not Great*, and avoid the over-use of Latin and terms like "strawman" and "Nirvana fallacy". (Writing over-much in Latin and over-using or mis-using terms like "strawman" does not so much make you look intelligent as kind of silly.) Just as some Christians are sometimes prone to over-quote from the Bible, some atheists are sometimes prone to over-quote Hitchens and Dawkins. I think we all value a nicely–stated original thought much more than a canned response, don't you?

Because I am writing this book from the perspective of a Christian Scientist-Unitarian Universalist-Humoristian, I'd like to, specifically, address those denominations for a moment.

When non-Humoristians are talking to Humoristians –

- Don't assume all Humoristians think, feel, and believe exactly the same about everything. Pretty much the only thing Humoristians have in common is the ability to laugh at themselves and the absurdity of life.

- The only effect pomposity, stodginess, self-righteous indignation, and sermonizing are going to have on a Humoristian is to get her laughing so hard she'll have tears pouring down her face. Unless that is the effect you're going for, don't waste your time with it.

When non-Unitarian Universalists are talking to Unitarian Universalists –

- Don't assume all Unitarian Universalists think, feel, and believe exactly the same about everything... because... I mean... these are Unitarian *Universalists*, for crying out loud! Trying to herd U-U members into one ideology would be like trying to herd cats.

- Don't waste your time trying to get U-U folks to get defensive about their religious beliefs. It ain't going to happen. Although you might see the U-U coming to the defense of social justice and freedom, you are not going to see them getting defensive about their religious beliefs because they don't have any to defend, really. So you can give THAT whole plot up right now.

When non-Christian Scientists are talking to Christian Scientists –

- Don't assume all Christian Scientists think, feel, and believe exactly the same about everything.
- Don't assume that because you were raised in another Christian denomination you are an expert on Christian

Science. There is a vast difference between fundamentalist Christianity, for instance, and Christian Science – as many fundamentalist Christians would be the first to point out.

- Do not assume that because you are the child of Christian Scientists you are an expert on Christian Science. (I am the daughter of a geologist, but I would not consider myself an expert on geology.)
- Don't assume because you read a Wikipedia article on Christian Science, or because someone once told you that they'd heard from someone else something about Christian Science, you are an expert on Christian Science. (I have actually been told by non-Christian Scientists to refer to Wikipedia to better find out what I believe as a

Christian Scientist. I have spent more than 50 years practicing this way of life, have led the services at my church, and written books about my experience with Christian Science. Do not tell me to go to Wikipedia to find out more about what I believe. Sheesh.)

- The "Christian Scientists are neither Christian, nor scientists" thing has gotten pretty old and is neither original nor helpful in maintaining thoughtful discourse. Let it go.

- Do not assume all Christian Scientists hold the same political or social beliefs. Christian Scientists are a pretty diverse group of people – there are Christian Scientists who are Democrats, Christian Scientists who are Republicans, Christian

Scientists who are liberal-progressives and Christian Scientists who are conservatives. Unlike some other religious institutions there is nobody in the Christian Science church who tells Christian Scientists how to vote. That is left up to individual conscience.

- Along the same lines, recognize that private Christian Science schools and institutions - and the people who are part of them - are not necessarily representative of the views and experience of every individual who is practicing Christian Science.
- Do not assume that because you know one Christian Scientist you know them all.
- Do not assume that Christian Scientists who go to doctors are not "real" Christian Scientists. For some Christian Scientists, Christian Science

is neither a religion nor an alternative health care system, it is a way of life – a way of looking at the world that has brought them healing and a lot of good.

When Christian Scientists are talking to non-Christian Scientists

- Avoid, if you can, using phrases like "working on a problem" or "the belief of" - most people are not going to understand what the heck you are talking about.
- Avoid, if you can, using absolutes. None of us have ascended, yet. Christian Scientists are still dealing with the same challenges as every other human being. Recognizing the common human experience we share with the rest of mankind is not a bad thing.

- It's alright to show natural human feeling – to cry, laugh, grieve. These are the feelings that connect us to the rest of humankind. Embrace them. Don't be afraid to bring human emotion into your conversations with others. Christian Scientists are not automatons.

- Do not talk down to others. Being a Christian Scientist doesn't make you any better, wiser, or more spiritually-minded than anyone else.

- Don't be afraid to laugh at yourself now and then, and don't be afraid to let others laugh at you, too. Recognize that to people unfamiliar with Christian Science some of the teachings found in Christian Science might seem completely ludicrous. And that's okay.

Okay. I guess that's pretty much all I have to say about that.

"Radical Reliance on Truth"

"I'm not going to be anybody's puppet, particularly not my own."
– Douglas Adams

"You are interested in Christian Science," said Markie, handing her a duster… she had found a book upon Christian Science in Jane's room when she went in to make the bed. "Yes," said Jane. "At least I don't know much about it. I just thought it might help to— to clear up something in my mind." "Perhaps it may," agreed Markie. "There was a mistress at Wheatfield House who practiced Christian Science and she had an extremely lucid mind…" Here Markie knelt down upon the hearth rug and began to lay the fire in the empty grate. "She was agreeable and cultured," continued Markie. "I liked her very much and I was much interested in her conversation." "Did she convert you?" Jane asked. "No, dear. If I have a pain I just take

*an aspirin in a little water. There is no need
to bother God about it."*
                    - D.E. Stevenson

*The tender word and Christian
encouragement of an invalid, pitiful patience
with his fears and the removal of them, are
better than hecatombs of gushing theories,
stereotyped borrowed speeches, and the
doling of arguments, which are but so many
parodies on legitimate Christian Science,
aflame with divine Love.*
                    – Mary Baker Eddy

Recently a fellow Christian Scientist made a comment on one of my blog posts that got me to thinking (which is always a good thing, right?).

Don wrote: *"Mrs. Eddy pushes us to have 'radical reliance' on God - an impossible order if one wishes to be 'fat and happy' in matter, too. Consequently, some individuals find ourselves taking a 'halting and halfway position' in our religion and at that point begin accepting all sorts of logic that veers away from true Christian Science. Loving our fellowman who has opposing views doesn't mean 'getting in bed with him.' ...Medicine is a mind-science. Christian Science is Mind (God) Science. There is a dramatic and opposite difference between the two, and we must be careful to keep both feet solidly grounded in that 'Science' which does bless us and the world–in spite of how illogical it seems to the materialist or to those of us who want to 'play nice' with the world. It all boils down to our responsibility, and it can't be shirked forever by any one of us. We must take a stand for Truth (God) if we wish to grow out of mortality using the same conviction as is recorded in Psalms 'Some trust in chariots, and some in horses: but we will remember the name of the Lord our God.' (Ps 20:7)'"*

Don's post got me to thinking about just what "radical reliance on Truth" actually means. Is "radical reliance on Truth" simply a euphemism for "avoiding the use of traditional medical science"? Or does "radical reliance on Truth" mean something else entirely – something bigger, something more?

Don got the phrase "radical reliance on Truth" from the textbook for Christian Science, *Science and Health with Key to the Scriptures,* authored by Mary Baker Eddy. Eddy writes: "Only through radical reliance on Truth can scientific healing power be realized." In the textbook, Eddy also writes: "If we would open their prison doors for the sick, we must first learn to bind up the broken-hearted. If we would heal by the Spirit, we must not hide the talent of spiritual healing under the napkin of its form, nor bury the morale of Christian Science in the grave-clothes of its letter."

I'm thinking that we need to be careful not to bury the talent of spiritual healing under the "napkin of its form." Whatever means a person chooses to use for healing – whether it's naturopathy, traditional medical science, Christian Science treatment, or something else – that's the form, the means, the method. The morale, or essence, of spiritual healing is Love - Love is the power that heals and transforms us. The God I follow – Love, Truth, Life, Principle, Mind, Soul, Spirit (synonyms Mary Baker Eddy, the discoverer

of Christian Science, gave for "God") – isn't
concerned with what kind of treatment we
choose to use – Love is going to remain
unchanging Love, and Truth is going to
remain unchanging Truth, no matter what
form or method we use for physical healing.
Truth doesn't have an opinion on which
form of treatment is best for treating disease
– because Truth doesn't know anything
about disease, to begin with. Truth knows
only perfection. And Truth and Love are
synonyms, so doesn't "radical reliance on
Truth" also mean "radical reliance on
Love"?

"Material methods are temporary,
and are not adapted to elevate mankind,"
wrote Eddy, and "If Christian Scientists
ever fail to receive aid from other Scientists,
– their brethren upon whom they may call, –
God will still guide them into the right use
of temporary and eternal means. Step by
step will those who trust Him find that 'God
is our refuge and strength, a very present
help in trouble'… Christ, Truth, gives
mortals temporary food and clothing until
the material, transformed with the ideal,
disappears, and man is clothed and fed

spiritually… Emerge gently from matter into Spirit. Think not to thwart the spiritual ultimate of all things, but come naturally into Spirit through better health and morals and as the result of spiritual growth."

When I choose to use Christian Science for healing I know my thought is going to be "elevated" by the experience, I know I'm going to gain a greater understanding of God and of who I am as Her child, and I know I will be transformed – not merely healed physically – but transformed.

I choose to turn to Christian Science for healing because it's simple, natural, uncomplicated, and spiritually-elevating, and it's always available to me no matter where I am, or who I'm with, or what scrape I've gotten myself into "this time". I choose to use my understanding of Christian Science to bring me healing because it has been proven to work for me.

My motives for choosing Christian Science treatment for healing have nothing to do with a fear of what other Christian Scientists are going to think of me, or because I'm concerned God's going to be angry at me, or because I'm worried about being ex-communicated, or because I'm opposed to something else, or because I'm scared of medical science, or feeling angry, self-righteous, or smug. My motive for turning to Christian Science for healing isn't because I feel the need to take a "stand for Truth" – Truth doesn't need me to take a stand for it – it's not in some battle it might lose – Truth was Truth yesterday, and will remain Truth tomorrow – and nothing I do is going to change that. Truth doesn't need me to side with it to continue to be Truth.

I use Christian Science because it's natural for me to do so – it's natural for me to draw my thoughts close to Love, to wrap myself up in the power of Truth, to free my thoughts to dance in the celebration of Life. And it's natural for me to experience healing by doing so.

And THAT is radical, man!

Students are advised by the author to be charitable and kind, not only towards differing forms of religion and medicine, but to those who hold these differing opinions. Let us be faithful in pointing the way through Christ, as we understand it, but let us also be careful always to "judge righteous judgment," and never to condemn rashly.

– Mary Baker Eddy

"Imagine No Religion"

"Are you a Bokononist?" I asked
him.

*"I agree with one Bokononist idea. I
agree that all religions, including
Bokononism, are nothing but lies."*

"Will this bother you as a scientist,"
*I inquired, "to go through a ritual like
this?"*

*"I am a very bad scientist. I will do
anything to make a human being feel better,
even if it's unscientific. No scientist worthy
of the name could say such a thing."*
– Kurt Vonnegut

*I find the whole business of religion
profoundly interesting. But it does mystify
me that otherwise intelligent people take it
seriously."*
- Douglas Adams

*Unrequited love and too much
church had worn out and subdued the gay
young man out of all recognition.*
- D.E. Stevenson

Our Master taught no mere theory,
doctrine, or belief. It was the divine
Principle of all real being which he taught
and practised. His proof of Christianity was
no form or system of religion and worship,
but Christian Science, working out the
harmony of Life and Love.
- Mary Baker Eddy

I have finally come to terms with the fact that I am just not a very religious person - at least not in the traditional sense of the word. I do not like meetings. I do not like busy work. I do not like being on committees. I hate dogma and nonsensical ritual and am not interested in debating which version of the *Bible* should be used at services – if something doesn't come from Love or lead to Love, I have no patience, time, or interest in it. I do not like being lumped in with every other person who calls himself or herself a Christian Scientist. I am not comfortable with the expectation (held by both non-Christian Scientists and some who call themselves Christian Scientists, too) that I will hold the exact same opinions

and beliefs as every other Christian
Scientist. I want no part of group-think.

I want to be allowed my own
experience in "earth's preparatory school",
to learn my own lessons, make my own
mistakes, and think my own thoughts. I want
to have the freedom to question and explore
and discover.

For me, Christian Science is much
more than a religion, and much more, too,
than some alternative health care system.
Christian Science is a way of life – a way of
looking at the world – and it has brought me
a lot of good – physical healings, freedom
from fear of lack and limitation, proof of the
power of Love and Truth. For me, Christian
Science isn't just some philosophical
mumbo-jumbo ideology – I have been able
to apply my understanding of Christian
Science in practical and useful ways in my
life.

A couple of months ago, for
instance, a loved one experienced "The
Week of Lost Things" (and I'm pretty sure
we've all gone through weeks like that,
right?) – keys, wallet, important papers
seemed to be continually disappearing.

Using my understanding of God, I was very quickly able to find these things for him – the most dramatic example being when I walked up to a chair, without hesitation or doubt, lifted up the cushion, and found his keys underneath. The loved one noted that there was no way I could have known he'd been anywhere near that chair when he'd lost his keys (it was not his usual chair), and no way I could have known where to begin to look for them. But I had opened my thought up to the Consciousness of Truth – had known nothing was outside that consciousness, and nothing was ever out of place – and followed where I was led – to that chair.

Was it a religion that had led me to that chair? Was it a "system of beliefs"? Was it a ritual, creed, or doctrine that told me to lift up that cushion? Nope. It was a "knowing", not a belief - an understanding of the reality and harmony of all things - that led me to that chair, and led me to lift up the cushion.

In the textbook for Christian Science, *Science and Health with Key to the Scriptures*, Mary Baker Eddy defines

"Church" as "The structure of Truth and Love; whatever rests upon and proceeds from divine Principle. The Church" Eddy writes, " is that institution, which affords proof of its utility and is found elevating the race, rousing the dormant understanding from material beliefs to the apprehension of spiritual ideas and the demonstration of divine Science, thereby casting out devils, or error, and healing the sick."

I really like that part about "rousing the dormant understanding from material beliefs to the apprehension of spiritual ideas..." – and I believe that finding the keys, finding the new job, and finding my sanity are all illustrations of a waking consciousness – an awakening from the belief in limitation and loss to the apprehension of limitless, infinite possibility and opportunity. And none of that, in my opinion, has anything to do with some human institution.

Eddy writes, "Long prayers, superstition, and creeds clip the strong pinions of love, and clothe religion in human forms. Whatever materializes worship hinders man's spiritual growth and keeps

148

him from demonstrating his power over error." She writes, "Christianity as Jesus taught it was not a creed, nor a system of ceremonies, nor a special gift from a ritualistic Jehovah; but it was the demonstration of divine Love casting out error and healing the sick, not merely in the name of Christ, or Truth, but in demonstration of Truth, as must be the case in the cycles of divine light."

Pure religion and undefiled before God and the Father, is this, To visit the fatherless and widows in their affliction, and to keep himself unspotted from the world.
- James 1:27

Creeds, doctrines, and human hypotheses do not express Christian Science; much less can they demonstrate it.
- Mary Baker Eddy

"Smile Because It Happened"

*In the grand, in the timeless, in the
chrono-synclastic infundibulated way of
looking at things, I shall always be here. I
shall always be wherever I've been.*
       - Kurt Vonnegut

*This man knew... he knew what it
was like to be separated from the one person
on earth by a dark, mysterious wood and a
high, stony mountain. I was not alone in my
experience - not alone anymore. The mere
fact that another had walked where I was
walking made the path easier for my feet.
The mere fact of finding a simile for the
mystery which separated me from my love
made it easier to bear.*
       - D.E. Stevenson

*He was now six light-years from the
place that the Earth would have been if it
still existed. The Earth. Visions of it swam
sickeningly through his nauseated mind.
There was no way his imagination could feel
the impact of the whole Earth having gone,
it was too big... He tried again. America, he*

150

thought, has gone. He couldn't grasp it. He
decided to start smaller again. New York
has gone. No reaction. He'd never seriously
believed it existed anyway. The dollar, he
thought, has sunk for ever. Slight tremor
there… McDonald's, he thought. There is no
longer any such thing as a McDonald's
hamburger. He passed out.
- Douglas Adams

I was looking through old photos today and came upon some pictures of the sons as toddlers and youngsters. Oh my gosh, those precious little faces! – rounded cheeks, rascally grins – their expressions of delight at being alive! There's the youngest one wearing a cowboy hat for a school play, peeking around the shrubbery with an impish smile, wearing an astronaut Halloween costume while he sits on my lap, painting a picture at the dining room table, napping with the family cat; And the oldest in his baseball uniform, riding his first bike, dressed as a fireman, riding the family dog like he's riding a horse, playing the piano at his first recital. The boys are all grown-up now and making their own lives. The days when I could strap them on my back and head off for a hike, or put them in the carrier on my bike and take them to the city park are gone.

And this is neither Christianly Scientific nor noble of me to admit this – but my heart is aching to hold those little boys close to me again.

It's not that I'm not glad to see the sons become independent, to see them launch themselves off into their own adventures and build their own lives – because I am, and I want them to find success, and I want them to get out and see the world beyond the borders of their little hometown. I don't want them to grow backwards like Benjamin Button.

But tonight, as I looked at the old photos, I wanted to have them with me at ALL of their ages.

And maybe someday the workings of quantum physics and metaphysics will help me see that I CAN have them at all of their ages.

But for now…

I guess I could find something in Mary Baker Eddy's writings that would be helpful to me. Or maybe Eckhart Tolle has something wise to say about this kind of thing. There's that verse in *Ecclesiastes* about there being a season for everything – that might work, I guess. But, actually, I think it's Dr, Seuss who has the answer for me tonight:

> *Don't cry because it's over, smile because it happened.*
> - Dr. Seuss

Amen.

Karen, do you want to turn around at all, or not?

There is no problem about changing the course of history— the course of history does not change because it all fits together like a jigsaw. All the important changes have happened before the things they were supposed to change and it all sorts itself out in the end.
- Douglas Adams

"Modern thought has progressed so enormously," said Ernest. "Dates are not considered so important nowadays; it's the background that really matters. It's understanding how the people lived, what kind of things they had to eat, and what they felt and thought."
- D.E. Stevenson

Last night – the night after grieving the separation in time from my toddler-sons - I had a dream about…. I think I was at a wedding – my friend, Teresa, married her Wesley last weekend and I think I'm still floating in the beauty and joy of that day.

In this dream I keep going from room to room in some building with a floor plan that never ends. I'm not feeling unhappy or scared or panicked – I'm just sort of walking along at a nice pace, not running from bad guys or anything. And periodically this voice – and in the dream I seemed to accept this voice was Teresa's – would ask me, "Karen do you want to turn around at all, or not?" And I would just start grinning when I heard the voice – like it was a joke or something.

When I woke up that question was still in my head. "Karen," I asked myself, "do you want to turn around at all, or not?"

And upon some reflection I decided that no, I did not want to turn around, thank you very much.

"Remember what happened to Lot's wife when she tried that?" I asked myself. "It did not go so well for her," I answered myself solemnly.

Which reminds me of the time… oh geeze, forgive me, dear reader, but I seem to have awakened chatty this morning. It happens sometimes. Prepare yourself for some rambling digressions and detours here…

Anyway… the story of Lot and his wife reminds me of the time last October when I was invited by a new friend to attend a Jewish service at her synagogue with her – she was providing the oneg Shabbat afterwards. I'd never been to a Jewish service before, and I was really excited about this opportunity.

The service was of the Reformed Jewish type - informal and friendly - we all sat in a circle and sang songs and heard stories.

One of the highlights, for me, was meeting the man with the tartan kippah. The kippah is the cap that the Jewish men wear to the service, and one of the men was wearing one made out of material that had a Scottish tartan pattern on it. It totally cracked me up. He started laughing when I asked him about it. He actually got the one he was wearing when he was visiting Israel - he's partly Scottish, and this tartan happened to match his Scottish family tartan!

The rabbi conducting the service was a young woman - attractive and funny, intelligent and kind – and one of the stories she read was the story of Lot and his wife – not the story as it's written in the *Bible*, but a Midrashim – one of the Jewish Midrash stories that explain the stories in the *Bible*. In the Midrashim that the rabbi read, Lot's wife was actually a sympathetic character who turned back because it broke her heart that her neighbors were being destroyed while she was escaping to safety. So, out of compassion, The Lord turned her into a pillar of salt so she could remain with her community.

I liked the story – it put a different spin on the story of Lot and his wife than the traditional interpretation and made me look at the story from a different perspective.

But this morning, for my purposes, I need to go back to the traditional interpretation of the story of Lot and his wife.

There is much in the *Bible* that Christian Scientists don't interpret literally. Christian Scientists don't believe the story of Adam and Eve is anything but an allegory, for instance. Christian Scientists don't believe the world was literally created in a week. And Mary Baker Eddy has this to say about how Christian Science interprets the Scriptures: "The Scriptures are very sacred. Our aim must be to have them understood spiritually, for only by this understanding can truth be gained. The true theory of the universe, including man, is not in material history but in spiritual development."

When I read the *Bible* what I see as a history major is the evolution and progress of society and mankind - gradually moving away from a god of war - a vengeful, angry, jealous anthropomorphic god - to God as, literally, Love. When I read the first chapter of *Genesis* I see the beauty of creation - I don't get hung up on the whole seven days and seven nights thing - Christian Scientists don't interpret that chapter literally - what I see is a creation made in God's image and likeness - beautiful and good and perfect. When I read the story of Adam and Eve, it's obvious to me that I'm reading an allegory. When I read the songs that David wrote I know I'm reading the words of a man who struggled with the same things I've struggled with in my life - I see his flaws and I see his mistakes and his victories, and I see him growing and maturing and I take comfort in that. Jesus' healings are evidence, for me, of the power of our thoughts, the power of love and good overcoming the challenges we all face - and they give me hope. *Revelations* is totally symbolic - in my mind, at least - showing the ultimate triumph of the things of the Spirit over the illusions of matter. For me, trying to interpret the Bible word-for-word in a literal way would be akin to trying to interpret Aesop's fables in a literal way.

So when I read the story of Lot and his wife in the *Bible* I'm not focused on a literal interpretation of that story – for me, it simply "does not compute" that the God I worship – Love – could be so furious at his children that he would violently and utterly destroy them. No, when I read the story of Lot and his wife what I'm looking for is what that story represents – what lesson or moral I might get from it and apply to my life.

And today the lesson I get from the story of Lot's wife is that I need to keep moving forward, to keep progressing, to not turn back and yearn for what *was*, but to look forward to what is to come - to trust that there's as much good ahead of me as there is good behind me. I mean… seriously… do I really want to freeze my sons in time? The graduation from university a couple weeks ago wouldn't have happened for the older son. The trip through Europe with his high school friends wouldn't have happened for the younger one. The future good they'll leave to the world would not be if they were frozen in toddler-hood. And that would really stink for the world. And for them. And for me, too.

> *…progress is the law of God, whose law demands of us only what we can certainly fulfill.*
> - Mary Baker Eddy

> *Brethren, I count not myself to have apprehended: but this one thing I do, forgetting those things which are behind,*

and reaching forth unto those things which are before, I press toward the mark for the prize of the high calling of God in Christ Jesus.

- Philippians 3

Taking a Break

I want to take a break, I said.
Can I step out of life for a moment,
or maybe stay in bed?
Can things go on without me awhile?
Can I just disappear?
Can you get on with your lives without me
and just pretend I'm not here?
For life is a messy business
and I'm tired and I am weary
I've made too many mistakes to count today
And I'd like to not make anymore, not any.

Will things get better?
Will life come out alright?
Will the hero find true love?
Will tomorrow be sparkly and bright?
Will there be a happy ending?
Will the ones I love know they're loved?
Will I see any more rainbows?
Will sun's rays beam through the clouds
above?

And the still, small voice reached into my
thought
- gentle, peaceable benediction -

"All the good you seek and all that you've
sought,
you can claim right now – and that' s no
fiction –
for Love is yours to express, to feel and to
be
you are wealthy beyond description.
Nothing else matters, there's no other power
no warring opinions, no need to cower.
You are loved and you're loving
and that's all there is to it
Love's loving child, and there's nothing else
but loving, simply nothing."

A Lesson in Love from a Little Girl

Oh, she says, well, you're not a poor man. You know, why don't you go online and buy a hundred envelopes and put them in the closet? And so I pretend not to hear her. And go out to get an envelope because I'm going to have a hell of a good time in the process of buying one envelope. I meet a lot of people. And, see some great looking babes. And a fire engine goes by. And I give them the thumbs up. And, and ask a woman what kind of dog that is. And, and I don't know. The moral of the story is, is we're here on Earth to fart around. And, of course, the computers will do us out of that. And, what the computer people don't realize, or they don't care, is we're dancing animals. You know, we love to move around. And, we're not supposed to dance at all anymore.

- Kurt Vonnegut, from an interview with David Brancaccio, *NOW (PBS)* (7 October 2009)

The other day on my walk in Bellingham I stepped into the local gelato store and ordered myself a treat. Normally, once I've been handed my gelato, I just continue on my walk. But this time I decided to sit at a table by the door and eat my gelato inside.

Not long after I sat down this couple – by their clothing, they looked like they might have been from India – walked in with a little girl of about three. The little girl looked at me, got this huge smile on her face, and her eyes lit up like she knew me – then she put out her arms for a hug. "Hi, sweetie!" I said, giving her a hug, "How are you doing?" And she hugged me back and went with her parents to get her gelato.

When she sat down with them, she kept looking over at me and grinning, and waving, and covering her mouth the way you do when you're excited. Simple unencumbered, unpretentious friendliness and joy just shined out from her like the sun. Before I left I went up to her parents and told her how precious their little daughter was and what her huge hug had meant to me. The mother smiled and said, "She really likes people."

That little girl's innocent, open friendliness really touched my heart. Her unquestioning acceptance of me as her friend – as someone she would like to hug – was very cool – a spontaneous expression of God, bursting with fearless Love.

Beloved children, the world has need of you,—and more as children than as men and women: it needs your innocence, unselfishness, faithful affection, uncontaminated lives.
- Mary Baker Eddy

Theresa, Akkima, and the Man in the Fairy Wings

I knew that it would be a pleasure to write for you... You do not remember me, of course - how could you remember - since the only time I ever saw you was three years ago, riding down Piccadilly on the top of a bus... You thanked the shabby stranger for rescuing a bunch of wild flowers which had fallen under the seat and you said, somewhat apologetically, "I am taking them to a country woman who lives in a basement. She likes country flowers best, you see."... I realized at once that you understand things; you were of the understanding kind...
- D.E. Stevenson

As a young child, Mom suffered heart damage as a result of rheumatic fever. Apparently doctors advised her to live a quiet and sheltered life. Mozzy did not do such a good job with that. Through the years she climbed Mount Rainier (twice), got married, birthed and raised three children, traveled, sang, gardened, hiked, and tended to her menagerie of goats, llamas, cats, and poodles. She maybe didn't do what she'd been told to do by her childhood physician, but she did what she needed to do to make a full and satisfying life for herself.

Eighty years after the rheumatic fever, Moz finally underwent open heart surgery to repair her heart. Before the surgery she underwent tests to determine if it was safe, at her age, to do this kind of invasive and intensive procedure. When the test results came back they indicated that, as her lead doctor put it, Moz had "the arteries and veins of someone in her twenties" and it was decided to go ahead with the operation.

As Love would have it, the surgery took place in the one May I wasn't tied down by a job or other obligations in twenty years – the spring that I left my public school career (and just a week or two after I'd published the *Middle Book*). I'm so grateful I could totally focus on Moz and could be with my dad and brothers during the surgery and Moz's recuperation without having to prepare for a substitute and prepare lesson plans.

The surgery was performed at a hospital two hours to the south of where I live. When I was booking a room in a hotel near there - The Inn at Gig Harbor - I mentioned that I was going to be there to be close to a dear family member while she underwent open heart surgery. The woman making the reservation for me got quiet for a moment. When she spoke again it was to tell me that she would be giving me a discount on my room, and she said that there was a suite, that was "just sitting there" and not being used that had a Jacuzzi in it, and she was going to put me in that room because she figured I'd need a Jacuzzi. I was speechless for a moment - overcome by her kindness and generosity.

When, a couple of days later, I drove down to the hotel to check in, I was very excited to meet Theresa Ready - the woman who had taken such good care of me in reserving my room. Her daughter was at the desk, and she told me she'd get her mom for me. Theresa came out of the back room to meet me, and she had tears in her eyes as she smiled at me. "No one ever asks to see me," she said, "I'm just an accountant." That cracked me up. This woman who was "just an accountant" was, it was obvious to me, a woman of great love and compassion, and I felt really privileged to meet her. We hugged, and she wished me all the best for my mom, and said she'd pray for her.

I had to leave for the hospital at 4:30 the next morning, and, knowing I would miss breakfast, the hotel packed up a box full of muffins, scones, yogurt, and juice to get me through the morning.

I wore my sparkly green fairy wings into the hospital - I knew Moz would get a kick out of that - she and I share the same sense of humor about stuff - and, sure enough, she started laughing as soon as she saw me. My brothers and dad were there, too, and we encircled our dear one with love and the confidence that all would be well.

The next eight hours passed in kind of a blur. Probably anyone who's been in the hospital for any length of time understands what I mean by that. It's a kind of surreal atmosphere - long stretches of wandering, chatting, reading, and - in these modern times - connecting to the hospital's free Wi-Fi to communicate with the outside world -

punctuated by quick, intense moments when an update comes through. Time disappears.

It was a sunny day, and there were several times when I needed to escape from the confines of the hospital and get some fresh air and sunshine, and see what was going on in the world outside. On one of my escapes, I walked several blocks into the sun, past a school, and to a community garden. There were a couple of women in the garden - one of them planting seeds, and the other taking pictures of her - and I asked them if it would be okay if I opened up the gate and came inside. They looked at me and smiled and welcomed me in. And this is when I met Akkima, the photographer. Akkima was a student at the University of Washington, Tacoma Campus, majoring in Media. Her assignment that day was to photograph her friend, the gardener. I told Akkima that I'm married to a photojournalist, and that I, too, have recently gotten interested in photography, and we shared our mutual enjoyment of capturing images and talked about that for a while. And, of course, we had to take pictures of each other.

Back in the hospital, I was reluctant to move from the lobby - there was a fountain and windows to the outside and sunshine - but eventually those of us who hadn't yet moved into the hospital's surgical waiting room joined our other family members there and settled in to await news.

There was another family, in the space next to us, also awaiting news about their loved one. I was impressed by how well-behaved the little children were while they waited. Frankly, they seemed to be doing better than me. I'm not very good at sitting and waiting in somber silence. This is not to say I don't appreciate quiet and stillness - because I do, for sure - but not when there's interesting people around me - I have a yearning to find out about them and make a connection with them - and this family waiting next to us was interesting.

I brought my glittery green fairy wings up to the little girl and asked her if she'd like to put them on for a while - she shyly shook her head no - she wanted no part of the fairy wings. However, the young man standing next to her agreed to put on the fairy wings for me. I'm not sure how old he was - my guess would be early twenties - and let's just say that he was not built the way one would picture a typical fairy is built. He and I and his entire family started cracking up when he allowed me to put those wings on him.

I'm happy to say that not long after he donned the fairy wings for me, the young man and his family heard good news about their grandmother's operation. It had gone well, and things were looking good.

Eventually, we learned that the surgery for Mozzy was finished, and that, although she wasn't out of the woods, yet, things were looking good for her, too.

My family and I went up to Moz's room after the operation - when she was still unconscious and sedated. I started singing some of her favorite hymns from *The Christian Science Hymnal* to her. "Oh dreamer, leave thy dreams for joyful waking..." I sang (to the tune of "Oh, Danny Boy") and then, joking, I asked her, "Wasn't that beautiful?" and - much to the surprise of all of us - she nodded her head twice! I think this is when I knew everything was going to be alright. "And for my next number..." I

173

said, and I'm pretty sure she was trying to laugh.

Moz was back!

Kinship with Womankind

*Divine Love always has met and
always will meet every human need.*
– Mary Baker Eddy

*Barbara tried to talk and dress at the
same time but she was not used to it, having
been an only child with no sisters to initiate
her in the art.*
- D.E. Stevenson

I am surrounded by menfolk:
Husband, sons, brothers, father. Beyond my
dear mother, I have few female relations in
my immediate family – I wasn't raised with
sisters, and I have no daughters. And though
I love the men in my family and feel really
blest by their presence in my life, there have
been times, now and then, when I've felt a
yearning for more female companionship in
my life. There are times when I've longed to
have someone with whom I can talk about
feminine stuff – flower gardens and
butterflies and baby things and goals and
dreams and books and movies and human
relationships. There's only so much

"basketball", "football", or "baseball" that I want to talk, you know? And I'm not much interested in machines – cars and motorcycles are useful means of transportation for me, but I don't have any kind of passion for them as the men-folk in my life seem to have.

There was a time last year – during winter - when I was feeling a real yearning for some female kinship. I put some prayerful thought into my feelings of isolation and loneliness – worked to know that everything I needed was always being supplied me by my Father-Mother God, and then let it go – in other words, opened my heart up to the infinite possibilities and let go of the feelings of lack and limitation.

And within days my beautiful niece, Claire, sent me a Facebook message to see if we could get together for a day during her winter break from university. As has so often happened in the last few years, this gift came completely out of the blue – there is no way I could have seen that one coming – but it was exactly what I needed!

Claire and I spent a day in Seattle together – we went to the butterfly exhibit at the Seattle Science Center, ate cheesecake at the Cheesecake Factory, and talked about books and movies and goals and dreams. I had so much fun that day.

For me, this was just another proof of the power, purpose, and manifestation of Love meeting "every human need."

Lessons from Samantha the Wonder Dog

*An old sign on the main gate said
BEWARE OF THE DOG, beneath which
someone had scrawled, "Why single out the
dog particularly?"*
- Douglas Adams

*Nell wagged her feathery tail. It was
good when the goddess descended from the
clouds and spoke to you; it gave you a cozy
safe feeling in your inside.*
- D.E. Stevenson

*When Rumfoord announced that he
was taking a perfectly tremendous dog
along, as though a space ship were nothing
more than a sophisticated sports car, as
though a trip to Mars were little more than a
spin down the Connecticut Turnpike—that
was style.*
- Kurt Vonnegut

This story starts with a phone call
from the Humane Society. My husband
called to tell me that he and the son were
bringing home a puppy. "A lab mix," he told

me. When the door opened and the puppy scampered into the home I realized that the words "lab mix" did not do this puppy justice.

"Sweetie," I said, looking at the puppy's humongous paws, "I think we're looking at something else entirely here."

The pup grew. And grew. AND GREW. Within a few months she'd grown into her feet and we found ourselves with what appeared to be a thoroughbred racehorse/big goof hybrid. Setting Sam loose in the house was like setting loose a miniature tornado. (Sam, of course, considered herself a lap dog. And we have the pictures to prove it – her long body hanging over the son's lap, a happy puppy-grin on her beautiful Labradane face.)

As a family we'd only ever owned mature, fully-grown dogs. A puppy was a new adventure for us.

The first time I took her for a walk on the Bellingham boardwalk was a real learning experience for me. She hadn't taken three steps when she deposited a mountain of poop on the trail. I think she must have been saving it up for just this kind of special

179

occasion. I dealt with her gift as quickly and delicately as was possible and continued on with our walk. She was probably only three months old then, but even at three months old she was an exuberant handful for me. She wanted to play with every human, dog, and contraption that crossed our path. She wanted to go this way – no, that way – no, this way – no, in circles – and I found myself constantly tugging and pulling and unwinding myself from her leash. It was exhausting.

Have I ever mentioned that I am a cat person? Cats are easy. You feed them a couple times a day, maintain a clean litter box for them, pet them now and then, let them curl up on your lap, and then they go off and entertain themselves in a mostly quiet and covert way. You're never really sure what they've got themselves up to when they're out of your sight, but you can trust it's probably not going to have the neighbors knocking on your door.

Samantha was very different from a cat.

When she escaped from her big fenced-in pasture – which happened twice or thrice – the neighbors appeared at our door. Without going into detail, let me just say, cryptically, that we once felt the need to drive a chicken to the vet to have repairs done to her gullet. The chicken survived. And an electric wire was added to Samantha's fence.

Scott is a responsible and devoted dog-owner. He signed Sam up for Dog Training Classes. Sam loved dog-training classes – they gave her an opportunity to show-off and get treats. Of course, when she didn't feel like showing-off and there weren't any treats to be had. Sam saw no reason to actually sit when asked to sit.

The day when I decided I could no longer take Samantha on walks in populated, public places was the day when she somehow managed to break away from the leash and went running off into the woods at Lake Padden in nearby Bellingham. I called, I cajoled, I pleaded. Every now and then she would spring out of the forest, a happy grin on her face, and then she'd dodge back into the woods. There was no way I could catch her, and no way I could get her to come to me. The situation looked pretty hopeless.

Then Samantha decided to go swimming in the lake, got herself out pretty deep, and tried to get out of the water and onto the dock. Her paws scrabbled against the wood, but could get no purchase. I could see she was struggling and hurried out on the dock to help her. When I got to her she looked up at me with a look of trust in her eyes – she knew I was going to help her. I reached over, yanked her out by the collar, and hooked her back onto the leash.

I was glad she was safe and back on the leash, and I decided that for her safety and mine it would be best to never get ourselves in that position again.

A couple years went by. Last summer I needed a hiking partner and eyed the now fully-grown Labradane speculatively. Would she, I wondered, knock me off the path and over a cliff? Run off into the woods and chase innocent wildlife? Decide to make friends with a bear? …Well… what the heck, right? You only live once. I hooked her onto the leash and away we went. I had a great day with

Sam. She stayed on the trail, and kept to my pace – only pausing now and then to sniff at interesting smells. She chased no bunnies or squirrels, and did not try to make nice with any bears.

That was our last big walk in a public place together until a month or so ago.

That is when I decided it was time to take Samantha back to the Bellingham boardwalk. My approach this time was different than the first time I took her on the boardwalk. This walk wasn't about me. It was about Sam. It was a walk for her. I was in no hurry, had no place I needed to be, nothing I was desperate to see. Sam, I decided, would choose how fast we went and how often we stopped. If other dogs approached I would pull her over and wait to see if the other dogs were willing to touch noses in a civil way, and then I'd watch and see how Samantha responded to that. If the situation started to get out-of-control, I would just load Sam back up in the car – without any anger – and bring her home.

I discovered that day that Sam had grown up from the exuberant big-footed puppy she'd been four years ago. She had no interest in jumping on little children. Wasn't interested in dogs who weren't interested in her. Stopped periodically to sniff and investigate, but didn't pull or yank on the leash. And when she needed to poop, she found a place off to the side in tall grass – and I was prepared and able to discreetly contain it in a plastic bag. The highlight of the excursion for her, I suspect, was when she met up with another dog a little bigger than herself – it looked sort of like a picture of a Leonberger that I found on the internet – and she and this new friend banged their chests together and barked happily at each other and had a generally great time going in circles around each other.

I learned some lessons that day: Sometimes it is Sam's turn to make the choices; Sometimes the walk is all about *her*; Sometimes what I want is to give Samantha what *she* wants. Samantha is making me a better human.

Besides the Adams books, the Vonnegut books, and the Stevenson books, another book I really enjoyed reading this year was *Kinship With All Life* by the author, J. Allen Boone. *Kinship With All Life* is really thought-provoking. It inspired me to try to look at my fellow creatures in a new way – not down on them, but horizontally. Boone talks about the difference between an animal *trainer* and an animal *educator*. A trainer uses the "make 'em or break 'em technique" – employing a reward-and-punishment process with the animal. But the educator is entirely different. Boone writes: "The animal *educator* does just the reverse of all this. Moving into the situation with insight and intuition, he places full emphasis on the mental rather than on the physical part of the animal. He treats it as an intelligent fellow being whose capacity for development and expression he refuses to limit in any direction." Writing about Larry Timble's technique in transforming the movie dog Strongheart into the star he became, Boone writes: "Trimble discovered that deep within the big combat dog, but solidly imprisoned there, was a wealth of magnificent character qualities. Those talents and graces, buried beneath the dog's tough physical exterior, did not need to be developed but liberated. That is what Trimble proceeded to do."

And that, I believe, is what we should do for all our furry friends.

Books! Books! Bring Me More Books!

"No," said Castle the elder. "For the love of God, both of you, please keep writing!"
- Kurt Vonnegut

Sarah lay back in her chair and laughed and laughed. Who on earth could have written this book?
- D.E. Stevenson

Whatever furnishes the semblance of an idea governed by its Principle, furnishes food for thought. Through astronomy, natural history, chemistry, music, mathematics, thought passes naturally from effect back to cause. Academics of the right sort are requisite. Observation, invention, study, and original thought are expansive and should promote the growth of mortal mind out of itself, out of all that is mortal. It is the tangled barbarisms of learning which we deplore, - the mere dogma, the speculative theory, the nauseous fiction.
- Mary Baker Eddy

Do you go through book phases, too?

Dr. Seuss was my first favorite author (and remains one of my favorites today). In the summer before second grade, my mom enrolled me in a Seuss-book-of-the-week club, and every day I'd run out to the mailbox to see if a new Seuss book had arrived for me. I learned to read with Seuss.

In third grade I had a wonderful teacher named Mrs. Malmstrom who introduced us to books that were full of great messages and imagery - *The Wrinkle in Time*, *Pippi Longstockings* – and in fourth grade Mr. Whittle introduced us to *The Hobbit*. I also remember reading and loving the *Mary Poppins* books and Laura Ingalls Wilder's books about life as a pioneer girl.

When I was in my teens I enjoyed science fiction (Isaac Asimov was my fave), romantic adventures by Rafael Sabatini (author of *Captain Blood*) and Baroness Orczy (*The Scarlet Pimpernel*), and the wit and insight I found in Mark Twain's books. And at the university I was huge into fantasy – Tolkien's trilogy, Peter S. Beagle's *The Last Unicorn*, and my friend, Renee, introduced me to the magic found in Frances Hodgson Burnett's *The Little Princess.*

In my twenties I enjoyed cozy murder mysteries by Agatha Christie and *You Are the Adventure* by J. Allen Boone, and gorged myself on edifying, moralistic stuff – books about noble-minded people doing really noble things and thinking really noble thoughts. In my thirties and forties I was big into Regency romances (you know - the ones involving rakish dukes and smartass governesses and a lot of humor) – interwoven with darker thrillers by Dean Koontz, P.D. James, Robert Ludlum, Jeffrey Archer, Margaret Atwood, and Ken Follett.

When I turned 51 and began working my way through The Year of Insanity there were several books that were very helpful to me – *The Secret Garden* by Frances Hodgson Burnett (whenever I'd get to the part about the arrival of spring and the uncle waking from his depression I'd start tearing up with the beauty of it), Eckhart Tolle's *The Power of Now*, Edward A. Kimball's *Lecture and Articles on Christian Science*, and Henry Drummond's *The Greatest Thing in the World* – a sermon on Love.

And once I'd made it through The Year of Insanity I found I no longer had any interest in fictionalized political thrillers or moralistic tomes or stories featuring rakish dukes. I needed something real. I needed literature I could sink my teeth into. I found myself reading old classics I'd somehow missed before – *To Kill a Mockingbird, A Separate Peace, The Red Badge of Courage, The Pearl* – and I found myself drawn to new classics – *The Help, Water for Elephants, The Life of Pi, The Kite-Runner, The Aviator's Wife.* My soul was craving the messages and inspiration found in the lives of real people, too – *Kon Tiki, Hiroshima, Night, Narrative of the Life of Frederick Douglass, The Boy Who Harnessed the Wind, The Boys in the Boat, Born to Run, Miracle in the Andes: 72 Days on the Mountain and My Long Trek Home; Strength in What Remains, Mountains Beyond Mountains, Touching the Void, Dark Summit, Kinship with All Life.* And I read some really thought-provoking books that challenged me to look at life from different perspectives: Michael Shermer's *Why Darwin Matters,* Margaret Laird's *Christian*

Science Re-Explored, Robert Lanza's *Biocentrism*, and Norman Cousins's *Anatomy of an Illness.*

A couple of Christian Scientists have told me that they "don't have time" to read anything that isn't "authorized Christian Science literature." And... well... yeah. That kind of thought makes me really sad. I think when we isolate and insulate ourselves from other thoughts and perspectives our thoughts have a tendency to grow stagnant. I think we need to throw ourselves into the white water of thought – let our thoughts get fresh oxygen in them, let the stagnant stuff on the top get broken-up and churned away. I'm pretty sure Mary Baker Eddy would agree with me about this, too. She encouraged us to think. In *Science and Health* she writes, "The time for thinkers has come." And later in the Christian Science textbook she writes, "Whatever inspires with wisdom, Truth, or Love - be it song, sermon, or Science - blesses the human family with crumbs of comfort from Christ's table, feeding the hungry and giving living waters to the thirsty."

Happily, I'm pretty sure those Christian Scientists who only read "authorized Christian Science literature" are in the minority. I've discovered, for instance, a lot of fellow Christian Scientists who are huge into Douglas Adams and Kurt Vonnegut. I take this as a good sign for the Christian Science movement.

I like what Margaret Laird has to say about opening one's thoughts up to different viewpoints in her book *Christian Science Re-Explored*: "As Science, the man of imagination is absolutely neutral. This means he clings to no personal opinions but is always free to let Truth give him clearer vision. In other words, he acknowledges Truth to be the Principle in every concept. He does not regard another's point of view as needing either rejection or acceptance. He recognizes that dissent is often more creative, more stimulating to original thinking, than consent. This does not mean dissent from the standpoint of right or wrong, but dissent from the standpoint of a view of Reality other than one's own. Often a viewpoint that differs greatly from our own will do more to stoke the furnace of imagination than one with which we agree. The acceptance of another's point of view as right, or the rejection of it as wrong, would interfere with our own individual creativity."

I probably could fill a whole 'nother book with my thoughts on the books I've read during the course of my life. But I'd like to just talk here a little more about two books that I think have a strong correlation to Christian Science: *Anatomy of an Illness: As Perceived by the Patient* by Norman Cousins, *and Biocentrism: How Life and Consciousness are the Keys to Understanding the True Nature of the Universe* by Robert Lanza.

> *Home is the consciousness of good*
> *That holds us in its wide embrace;*
> *The steady light that comforts us*
> *In every path our footsteps trace.*
> – Rosemary Cobham, *Christian Science Hymnal Supplement*, #443

I very much enjoyed reading Robert Lanza's book, *Biocentrism: How Life and Consciousness are the Keys to*

Understanding the True Nature of the Universe. I found it thought-provoking and utterly fascinating. And as I was reading Lanza's book, I couldn't help but make comparisons between the ideas I was reading in it to the ideas found in Christian Science.

Lanza writes: "Take the seemingly undeniable logic that your kitchen is always there, its contents assuming all their familiar forms, shapes, and colors, whether or not you are in it... But consider: the refrigerator, stove, and everything else are composed of a shimmering swarm of matter/energy. Quantum theory... tells us that not a single one of those subatomic particles actually exists in a definite place. Rather, they merely exist as a range of probabilities that are unmanifest."

A little later, Lanza writes: "Three components are necessary for a rainbow. There must be sun, there must be raindrops, and there must be a conscious eye (or its surrogate, film) at the correct geometric location... your eyes must be located at that spot where the refracted light from the sunlit droplets converges to complete the required geometry. A person next to you will complete his or her own geometry... and will therefore see a separate rainbow... As real as the rainbow looks, it requires your presence just as much as it requires sun and rain." In other words, the answer to the question about whether a tree falling in a forest makes a sound if there's no one to hear it, is "no." A falling tree may make waves and vibrations, but an ear is needed to turn those waves and vibrations into sound. Lanza writes: "... without perception, there can be no reality."

In her book, *Science and Health with Key to the Scriptures*, Mary Baker Eddy writes: "Belief in a material basis... is slowly yielding to the idea of a metaphysical basis, looking away from matter to Mind as the cause of every effect." Eddy writes: "Metaphysics resolves things into thoughts, and exchanges the objects of sense for the ideas of Soul." And further in the book she writes: "As mortals gain more correct views of God and man, multitudinous objects of creation, which before were invisible, will become visible."

In *Biocentrism*, Robert Lanza points out that the "dividing line between self and nonself is generally taken to be the skin, strongly implying that I am this body and nothing else." But Lanza believes this is a myth. "Nothing," he writes, "is perceived except the perceptions themselves, and nothing exists outside of consciousness." According to Lanza then, we are directly connected to whatever we see, feel, and hear – it's not outside our consciousness, but a part of it – and there's no separation between what we perceive and what we are.

Mary Baker Eddy would agree that individuals are not isolated beings, separated from the rest of the universe, but she has a different take on our connectedness to each other, and to all. "When the divine precepts are understood, they unfold the foundation of fellowship, in which one mind is not at war with another, but all have one Spirit, God, one intelligent source, in accordance with the Scriptural command: 'Let this Mind be in you, which was also in Christ Jesus.' Man and his Maker are correlated in divine Science, and real consciousness is cognizant only of the things of God."

Of western religions – Christianity, Judaism, Islam – Lanza writes: "No mention is made of other states of consciousness, nor of consciousness itself... except in mystical sects..." Ahem. Well. Yeah. This is simply not true. In *Science and Health with Key to the Scriptures* (published in 1875 – long before Lanza arrived on Earth), Mary Baker Eddy, the founder of Christian Science (a way of life that its adherents consider "Christian" and not at all "mystical"), mentions "consciousness" 80 times.

But I suppose we can make a distinction between the consciousness Lanza is attempting to explain in his book, and the consciousness Eddy refers to in hers. Lanza talks about the structure of the brain, and a physical universe. Eddy speaks of a spiritual consciousness – the consciousness of Mind, God – and provides a practical use for drawing our thoughts near to that consciousness: "When we realize that Life is spirit, never in nor of matter, this understanding will expand into self-completeness, finding all in God, good, and needing no other consciousness."

"To succeed in healing," Eddy writes, "you must conquer your own fears as well as those of your patients, and rise into higher and holier consciousness."

Eddy provides us with a choice. She claims we can choose which consciousness, which perception, we want to accept as real in our lives – and that choice will determine our experience here. "Dear reader, which mind-picture or externalized thought shall be real to you, - the material or the spiritual? Both you cannot have. You are bringing out your own ideal. This ideal is either temporal or eternal. Either Spirit or matter is your model... If sin, sickness, and death were understood as nothingness, they would disappear. As vapor melts before the sun, so evil would vanish before the reality of good. One must hide the other. How important, then, to choose good as the reality!"

Foreseeing the future, Eddy wrote in 1875: "The mariner will have dominion over the atmosphere and the great deep, over the fish of the sea and the fowls of the air. The astronomer will no longer look up to the stars, - he will look out from them upon the universe; and the florist will find his flower before its seed. Thus matter will finally be proved nothing more than a mortal belief, wholly inadequate to affect a man through its supposed organic action or supposed existence. Error will be no longer used in stating truth. The problem of nothingness, or 'dust to dust,' will be solved, and mortal mind will be without form and void, for mortality will cease when man beholds himself God's reflection, even as man sees his reflection in a glass."

...within man is the soul of the whole; the wise silence; the universal beauty, to which every part and particle is equally related, the eternal ONE. And this deep power in which we exist and whose beatitude is all accessible to us, is not only self-sufficing and perfect in every hour, but the act of seeing and the thing seen, the seer and the spectacle, the subject and the object, are one. We see the world piece by piece, as the sun, the moon, the animal, the tree; but the whole, of which these are shining parts, is the soul.

- Ralph Waldo Emerson

Okay, there's one more book I read recently that I just need to share with you - Norman Cousins's book, *Anatomy of an Illness: As Perceived by the Patient*. It's a book that I've long suggested OTHER people read - because I'd heard it was amazing - but... ahem... I'd never actually read it myself. Now that I've read it, I am gratified to say that I was right in suggesting it to others.

For those of you who have never heard of *Anatomy of an Illness*, allow me to give a brief summary: Norman Cousins, a columnist for the *Saturday Review,* was stricken by a serious illness from which he was told by specialists he would never recover. He declined to accept this verdict for himself, and, with the support of his personal physician, Dr. William Hitzig, prescribed a form of treatment for himself.

The first thing he did was get himself moved out of the hospital and into a hotel room. He wanted to have peace and not be forced to fit into the routine of a hospital - constantly being awakened to have his sheets changed, to be fed processed hospital food, pricked with needles, injected with drugs, and to have his blood drawn multiple times when once would have been sufficient. He also put himself on a regimen of a high intake of ascorbic acid (vitamin C), and humor. He plied himself with old Allen Funt Candid Camera episodes and Marx Brothers movies and discovered that laughter had an anesthetic effect that would give him "at least two hours of pain-free sleep."

Norman Cousins was able to recover from his illness, and later the story of his illness and recovery was published in the *New England Journal of Medicine. Anatomy of an Illness: As Perceived by the Patient* picks up where the story published in the *NEJM* left off, and provides medical research, and communication and published tracts from medical professionals, that bring up the question of the importance of the "human touch" and positive emotions on patient recovery.

Cousins writes: "... long before my own serious illness, I became convinced that creativity, the will to live, hope, faith, and love have biochemical significance and contribute strongly to healing and to well-being. The positive emotions are life-giving experiences...There was also humor. Albert Schweitzer employed humor as a form of equatorial therapy, a way of reducing the temperatures and the humidity and the tensions. His use of humor, in fact, was so artistic that one had the feeling he almost regarded it as a musical instrument."

"I was also fortunate...," writes Cousins, "in having a doctor who believed that my own will to live would actually set the stage for progress; he encouraged me in everything I did for myself."

Anatomy of an Illness is broken into six chapters - the first chapter talks about his illness and recovery; the second chapter talks about the effect of placebos on health; the third chapter goes into the importance of creativity in living a long and healthy life; the fourth chapter talks about pain; the fifth chapter talks about Holistic Health; and the last chapter is entitled "What I Learned from Three Thousand Doctors".

In the chapter titled "The Mysterious Placebo" Cousins writes:

"It is doubtful whether the placebo - or any drug, for that matter - would get very far without a patient's robust will to live. For the will to live is a window on the future. It opens the individual to such help as the outside world has to offer, and it connects that help to the body's own capability for fighting disease. It enables the human body to make the most of itself... What we see ultimately is that the placebo isn't really necessary and that the mind can carry out its difficult and wondrous missions unprompted by little pills. The placebo is only a tangible object made essential in an age that feels uncomfortable with intangibles... The placebo, then, is an emissary between the will to live and the body. But the emissary is expendable. If we can liberate ourselves from tangibles, we can connect hope and the will to live directly to the ability of the body to meet great threats and challenges. The mind can carry out its ultimate functions and powers over the body without the illusion of material intervention."

Cousins talks about the need so many of us seem to have to see a doctor DOing something and giving us something tangible. But he suggests that there may come a time when these "tangibles" are no longer needed. As a Christian Scientist who's learned to turn immediately to Love, God, for healing, this thought really resonated with me.

Cousins goes on to talk about a meeting he had with the famous doctor and philanthropist, Albert Schweitzer, in the jungles of Africa where Schweitzer had set up a medical clinic. During dinner with Dr. Schweitzer he remarked that the people of the jungle were lucky to have the medical doctor in their midst so they didn't have to go to the local witch-doctors. Dr. Schweitzer asked Cousins how much he knew about witch-doctors, and Cousins had to admit he knew nothing, really. So the next day Dr. Schweitzer introduced Cousins to a witch-doctor and asked the witch-doctor if Cousins could watch him at work. As Cousins observed the witch-doctor he saw that his patients were, basically, provided one of three kinds of treatment - one group was given herbs to brew for tea, a second group was provided with an African incantation, and a third group was referred to Dr.

Schweitzer for treatment. Later Dr. Schweitzer suggested that those given herbs probably had problems that the witch-doctor recognized were functional, rather than organic; those provided with an incantation were suffering from psychogenic ailments which were treated by African psychotherapy; and the third group was suffering from serious physical problems that might require surgery.

Cousins writes: "When I asked Dr. Schweitzer how he accounted for the fact that anyone could possibly expect to become well after having been treated by a witch doctor, he said that I was asking him to divulge a secret that doctors have carried around inside them ever since Hippocrates.

"'But I'll tell you anyway," he said... 'The witch doctor succeeds for the same reason all the rest of us succeed. Each patient carries his own doctor inside him. They come to us not knowing the truth. We are at our best when we give the doctor who resides within each patient a chance to go to work.'

"The placebo is the doctor who resides within."

In the fourth chapter, entitled "Pain is Not the Ultimate Enemy", Cousins writes: "The most ignored fact of all about pain is that the best way to eliminate it is to eliminate the abuse. Instead, many people reach almost instinctively for the painkillers - aspirins, barbiturates, codeines, tranquilizers, sleeping pills, and dozens of other analgesics or desensitizing drugs... If ignorance about the nature of pain is widespread, ignorance about the way pain-killing drugs work is even more so. What is not generally understood is that many of the vaunted pain-killing drugs conceal the pain without correcting the underlying condition. They deaden the mechanism in the body that alerts the brain to the fact that something may be wrong. The body can pay a high price for suppression of pain without regard to its basic cause."

"The king of all painkillers of course, is aspirin... Aspirin is self-administered by more people than any other drug in the world. Some people are aspirin-poppers, taking ten or more a day. What they don't know is that the smallest dose can cause internal bleeding."

"Pain-killing drugs are among the greatest advance in this history of medicine... But their indiscriminate and promiscuous use is making psychological cripples and chronic ailers out of millions of people... Almost from the moment children are old enough to sit upright in front of a television screen, they are being indoctrinated into the hypochondriac's clamorous and morbid world. No wonder so many people fear pain more than death itself."

I found this chapter really interesting. As a person raised in Christian Science by my mother - and with an outdoor-adventure-loving mountain-climbing dad - there was not a lot of pill-popping going on in my home. I think I was pretty distracted from pain by all the fun stuff going on around me - all the hiking, bike-riding, tree-climbing, and laughter that filled my days. Who had the time to spend focused on scratched shins and bruised knees when there was a good game of tag to play, right? Fresh air, exercise, laughter, and learning how to bring my thoughts close to

Love, Truth, Life (God) seemed, for me, to be the best prescription for good health.

In the last chapter, "What I Learned from Three Thousand Doctors", Cousins describes the more than 3,000 letters he received from doctors following the publication of his story in the *NEJM*. Cousins writes: "What was most remarkable and gratifying about these letters was the evidence of an increasingly open attitude by many doctors to new and even unconventional approaches in the treatment of serious disease."

Cousins writes: ""Hundreds of letters from doctors... reflected the view that no medication they could give their patients was as potent as the state of mind that a patient brings to his or her own illness. In this sense, they said, the most valuable service a physician can provide to a patient is helping him to maximize his own recuperative and healing potentialities." He writes: "The rapid rise in the educational level of Americans was reflected in the ability of many people to inform themselves to a far greater extent than ever before about health matters. Many millions of Americans got into the habit of following medical developments. In their own relationships with physicians they no longer were disposed to accept medical decisions unquestioningly. They tended to evaluate doctors according to the willingness of the physician to enter into a mutually respectful dialogue with them."

"One of the most striking features that emerged from the letters I received from doctors is the evidence of a new respect for the ideas of nonprofessionals," Cousins writes. And then he quotes Dr. Gerald Looney, of the Medical College of the University of Southern California: "Nothing is more out of date than the notion that doctors can't learn from their patients... I teach my students to listen very carefully to their patients and to concerned and informed laymen. Good medical practice begins with good listening."

Near the end of the book, Cousins asks this question: "Is there a conflict at times between the treatment of disease and the treatment of human beings?" Whoaaah... what a great question, right?

The best medical practitioners, to my way of thinking, are the ones who are able to listen to their patients, reassure them, provide confidence, and treat their patients as human beings with needs beyond the physical. I have encountered several physicians like this - people who not only radiated a confidence in their own abilities, but recognized the worth and value of their patients' abilities, too, and treated them as respected partners in the healing process.

In a Christian Science treatment, of course, there is no question but that the patient is a partner. There are no hospital rooms, routines, and procedures for a patient to negotiate. No scary machines that beep at them. No life-threatening side effects from pharmaceuticals. And no need for a placebo, either. Christian Science treatment skips all the stuff that Cousins refers to as the "emissary between the will to live and the body" and the "illusion of material intervention." Well. Except for maybe a good Marx Brothers movie. Or maybe a Monty Python clip - now THAT's the kind of material intervention I can always use to feel better.

"One would be blind not to recognize that before and even after the advent of modern scientific medicine there were great and able healers of the sick who were not men of science, but who had the ability to reassure the patient and thus favorably to influence the course of the illness. It is also obvious that there have been excellent scientists who were very mediocre practitioners. Thus history teaches that any division of the science and art of medicine is necessarily harmful to practice."

- Arturo Castiglioni, *A History of Medicine* (as quoted in *Anatomy of an Illness* by Norman Cousins)

The hand that stocks the drug stores rules the world. Let us start our Republic with a chain of drug stores, a chain of grocery stores, a chain of gas chambers, and a national game. After that, we can write our Constitution.

-Kurt Vonnegut

"It all began, I said, when I decided that some experts don't really know enough to make a pronouncement of doom on a human being. And I said I hoped they would be careful about what they said to others; they might be believed and that could be the beginning of the end."
- Norman Cousins, *Anatomy of an Illness: As Perceived by the Patient*

Adventures in the Secret Garden

*Ernest was happy; the garden was
full of the late-afternoon golden sunshine
and the song of birds. It was quiet and
peaceful after the chatter of the tennis club.
The dew glistened on the grass like
millions of diamonds; a lark was singing
blithely. Ernest thought that he had never
enjoyed anything more deeply and perfectly
than that Early Celebration, his heart was
full of peace and happiness. It was too
wonderful to talk about.*
- D.E. Stevenson

*There's naught as nice as th' smell
o' good clean earth, exept th' smell o' fresh
growin' things when th' rain falls on 'em.*
- Frances Burnett Hodgson

Nature is a wonderful thing.
- Kurt Vonnegut

The other day I found some pictures
of my Secret Garden when it was brand
new. The photo showed five or six knee-
high shrubs and trees – vulnerable, but

plucky little infant flora planted in hopeful anticipation that one day they would be strong, sturdy grown-ups covered in flowers and making a nice little spinney for the neighborhood birds.

And they HAVE grown up! Today the baby shrubs and trees – the lilac bushes, mock orange, forsythia, flowering quince, and the hedge composed of wild rose, twin flowers, and snowberry bushes that I dug up from roadside ditches – have all grown together to create a REAL Secret Garden – a hidden floral cavern of sweet-smelling life.

It seems every week some new gift appears in there. First came the daffodils - their sunny little faces dancing bravely in the February winds. Then came the tulips - all cheery in red and pink and yellow. Soon after the tulips, lilac blossoms, and columbine appeared, waving their flower-flags to the world. And then a curtain of pastel clematis dropped in front of the opening to my garden - making it look like the portal to a fairy tale land. And now we've got roses and iris, honeysuckle azalea and peonies. I've got some magic growing out there.

Last week I spent most of a day reading a book, and sitting under the sweet-smelling canopy of cecil brunner roses that now arches over half of my Secret Garden. My cecil brunner rose bush has been in my family for more than 50 years - I transplanted it from my mom's garden about ten years ago. A couple years ago I wasn't sure it was going to make it - there were hardly any blooms and its foliage was thin and struggling. But this year! - I've never seen anything like it! - thousands and thousands of pale pink blossoms carrying their fresh, spicy scent, spill over the cedar rail fence, rise five or six feet over the little trellis that was meant to give it support, and arch over my garden into the butterfly bush. I sat in the dappled shade of my tent of roses, and listened to the wind in the cotton woods, and the birdsong, and breathed in the scents - the roses, the honeysuckle azalea, the iris, the smell of dried grass - and just felt full of the Goodness of Life.

There's a little bunny that pays me a visit every now and then in the Secret Garden. He lets me sing a hymn to him - his nose twitching, his bunny ears flicking -

patiently waiting until I'm done before hopping on to the rest of his day.

Bees are busily buzzing away in the roses, and butterflies and hummingbirds and chickadees and robins and goldfinch give me the pleasure of using the flowers I've planted, and the birdfeeders I've set out for them.

Expressions of the Consciousness of Love everywhere!

The floral apostles are hieroglyphs of Deity. Suns and planets teach grand lessons. The stars make night beautiful, and the leaflet turns naturally towards the light.
- Mary Baker Eddy

And the secret garden bloomed and bloomed and every morning revealed new miracles.
- Frances Hodgson Burnett

"They are called harmoniums."

He knew he had been listening to the music of life itself. The music of light dancing on water that rippled with the wind and the tides, of the life that moved through the water, of the life that moved on the land, warmed by the light.
-Douglas Adams

The clear notes stirred something in his heart, something deep and elemental that had been slumbering for years. Mrs. Mildmay— on the other side of the road— heard the music also. It was music only in the sense that bird-song is music.
- D.E. Stevenson

Because of their love for music and their willingness to deploy themselves in the service of beauty, the creatures are given a lovely name by Earthlings. They are called harmoniums.
- Kurt Vonnegut

Near the beginning of my recent term as Reader we had a guest soloist – a

217

pretty young woman named Rhianna. Rhianna sang a song that day that I'd never heard before. It was called *In His Eyes,* by a woman named Mindy Jostyn, and it touched my heart and had me in sniffles.

Here are the words to the first verse:

In His eyes, you're a fire that never goes out

A light on the top of a hill

In His eyes you're a poet, a painter, a prophet

With a mission of love to fulfill

Outside there's a world so enchantingly strange

A maze of illusion and lies

But there's never a story that ever could change

The glory of you in His eyes

That day after church I went home and found out all I could about Mindy Jostyn and this song. I googled and learned that Jostyn, a Christian Scientist, had been a good friend of Carly Simon's and that she'd written *In His Eyes* for the Village Center for Care AIDS Day Treatment Center in New York City. I imagined Mindy Jostyn singing this song for AIDS patients, and thought about what the words must have meant to them.

I learned, too, that Mindy Jostyn had died several years before, when she was in her early forties, of cancer. She'd left behind two young sons and a devoted husband. I was sad that I hadn't known Mindy when she was here with us – I wished then that I could have been able to tell her how much I enjoyed her music.

I ended up buying Mindy Jostyn's *In His Eyes* CD and listened to Jostyn's music on the way to and from work every day for, like, three months before I finally replaced it with some other CD. It was the CD I brought to the Unitarian Universalist church service, and the song I asked Sally to play for the congregation. I was like Pavlov's dogs when it came to that song. All I had to hear was the opening chord and I was tearing up.

Near the end of my term as Reader, something really cool happened. Mindy Jostyn's brother and sister-in-law happened to come to our church for a visit. It was such a pleasure for me to meet them, and to be able to tell them both what Mindy's music had meant to me. Maybe I couldn't tell Mindy Jostyn what *In His Eyes* had meant to me, but I could tell her family, and that seemed just as good somehow.

Another musical artist I discovered in the last couple years is an amazing blues guitarist named Joe Bonamassa. Scott and I heard Bonamassa for the first time during a PBS pledge drive. My jaw literally dropped open when Bonamassa started his first song. I looked at Scott and Scott looked at me - our eyes huge - and within minutes we'd pledged our support to PBS and purchased tickets to a Bonamassa concert coming to Seattle in the spring – this would be how we'd celebrate our wedding anniversary.

Of course, one of the most important parts of any event is the anticipation leading up to it – and there was plenty of that. And once we got to Seattle there was something very fun about getting in a line with a bunch of exuberant fellow baby boomers – except for the gray hair and laugh lines, looking just like a bunch of excited teenagers in line for a Macklemore concert. It felt, to me, like we were with fellow travelers we'd known all our lives. Just being Bonamassa fans meant we probably had a lot in common – good taste in music being the chief thing, of course.

The concert was so fun! And there was something really amazing about sitting in a theatre full of other people caught up in the same tide of inspiration. There was power in that room.

I am one of those people who believes there's a meaning to life – a meaning greater than merely breathing, breeding, and consuming material things. And, for me, music and art – the things of Soul – are a part of what makes life meaningful. Ray Charles said, "I was born with music inside me. Music was one of my parts. Like my ribs, my kidneys, my liver, my heart. Like my blood. It was a force already within me when I arrived on the scene. It was a necessity for me - like food or water."

Yes.

Music is a moral law. It gives soul to the universe, wings to the mind, flight to the imagination, and charm and gaiety to life and everything.
– Plato

Music washes away from the soul the dust of everyday life.
- Berthold Auerbach

In Memory of Russ

I'm eighty-three and homeless. It was the same when World War II ended. The Army kept me on because I could type, so I was typing other people's discharges and stuff. And my feeling was "Please, I've done everything I was supposed to do. Can I go home now?" That's what I feel right now. I've written books. Lots of them. Please, I've done everything I'm supposed to do. Can I go home now?
- Kurt Vonnegut (*Rolling Stone*)

Before Scott and I were engaged, he asked me to visit his family on the east coast with him. This would be the first time I'd meet his parents and sisters.

Scott's parents lived, at that time, in New Milford, Connecticut. I'd never been to Connecticut before, but ever since I'd read Mark Twain's *A Connecticut Yankee in King Arthur's Court* in junior high, I'd hoped to one day go there. Scott was also going to take me to New York City for the first time, and I was looking forward to that. But the highlight of the trip would, of course, be meeting Scott's family. I was eager to meet them, and a little nervous, too. I really hoped they would like me.

I needn't have worried. Scott's family was very welcoming to me. His mom, Marilyn, and sisters were all kind and funny and beautiful, and his dad, Russ, totally cracked me up. I felt like I was looking at an older, slightly shorter, version of Scott when I looked at Russ – I remember seeing a picture of Russ in uniform back in World War II and the resemblance to Scott was uncanny (later a friend saw a copy of that picture in our home and remarked that she didn't know Scott had been in the Army).

Scott's siblings, his brother-in-law, Matt, and his little niece and nephew, were all at the family home when I visited, and, figuring it might be awhile before they were all in the same place at the same time again, they gathered together in the backyard for a family photo. My plan was that I would just stand off to the side and watch – seeing as how I wasn't a part of the family. But Russ would hear none of it. "But I'm not a part of your family – I don't want to ruin your family picture by putting myself in there," I tried to say – but Russ told me not to worry about that, and gently herded me into the front row.

And whoah. Just now, when I look back at that moment, I realize that was the moment when Scott and I became unofficially engaged.

Twenty or so years after we were married Scott's dad began showing signs of Alzheimer's. Marilyn was able to care for him in their home up until the last year or two, when he was moved into a care facility. We visited him there whenever we were back east.

Even at the end he was cracking me up. He did this weird trick with his eye – he could lower one eyelid without the other one squinting at all. And if anyone asked him a question, he would say, "Doh" and then get this expression on his face that had us all laughing. His humor was the essence of him, and it never left him.

Russ died a couple months after I'd started working at the alternative high school, and I took a week off to join Scott and his family in celebrating Russ's life. It was a precious time.

Russ was put to rest in the local cemetery in upstate New York just before the snows – on the last weekend before the cemetery closed for the winter. Russ had been stationed in Europe during World War II and was buried with full military honors. The Honor Guard appeared in uniform at the cemetery and solemnly draped his coffin with the American flag. I know that meant a lot to Marilyn, and to the rest of us, too.

The longer we live, the more good-byes we experience. Friends die. Family members die. Loved ones move away. The good-byes haven't gotten any easier for me. There are times when saying good-bye is really hard, isn't it?

But I guess for those of us left behind it's our job to keep our loved ones alive in our memories and thoughts and hearts. Those of us who had the good fortune to have Russ in our lives will always have him with us.

...if a friend be with us, why need we memorials of that friend?
- Mary Baker Eddy

Preparing for the Best

Sooner or later, Chrono believed, the
magical forces of the Universe would put
everything back together again. They always
did.
    – Kurt Vonnegut, *Sirens of Titan*

"It's turned out all right after all,"
she said contentedly. "Things usually do,
somehow. You worry and fuss and try to
make things go the way you think they
should, and then you find that the other way
was best. I'm going to try not to worry about
things anymore."
    - D.E. Stevenson

Two years ago, when I wrote *The*
Madcap Christian Scientist's Middle Book, I
could not have guessed that today I'd be
working where I'm working, or that I'd have
met the new friends I've met. I couldn't
have guessed that my pictures would be
published in *The Bellingham Review* or that
I'd take a sail on a tall ship. Two years ago I
hadn't yet read Kurt Vonnegut, D.E.
Stevenson, or Douglas Adams, and I hadn't

yet heard of Joe Bonamassa or Mindy Jostyn. Two years ago I hadn't had the great joy, yet, of watching my youngest son graduate high school, and my oldest son and niece graduate from university.

A lot has happened in the last two years!

Are there challenges? Are there ever days when I'd like to just step off the planet for a while and let the world carry on without me? You betcha. I still have moments of panic, fear, and worry. But I'm making progress and I'm learning. I've gotten better at taking life's challenges in stride. I'm learning not to worry so much about the "what ifs" until they happen, and learning that I have the spiritual resources to deal with them when they do.

I've sometimes heard people say that they were "preparing for the worst, but hoping for the best." There was a time when I didn't really question the idea of that – it seemed sort of sensible to me, I guess. But lately I've looked at that phrase in a different way. It's occurred to me that there have been times in my life when I was so afraid something good wasn't going to happen for me, that I mentally shut myself off from the hope of its possibility so I wouldn't be disappointed if it didn't happen In doing that, I missed out on the "expectancy of good" that is such an important part of living Christian Science. Not only was I "preparing for the worst" – I was expecting it.

Is there ever really a need to "prepare for the worst"? I suppose it might be prudent to spend a little time preparing for a possible emergency. If you live in San Francisco it might be helpful to you and your neighbors to be prepared for earthquakes. And if you live in Nebraska it might be considered common sense to know what to do if a tornado is headed your way. But just how much time should a person spend thinking about this kind of thing?

It's impossible, really, to prepare physically for every challenge that confronts us during our lives. But we *can* prepare mentally and spiritually so that when any type of challenge appears in our paths, we have the confidence and courage to deal with it.

One of my all-time favorite examples of this can be seen in the events of the Apollo 13 mission in 1970. Talk about courage and confidence under pressure. None of the NASA engineers involved in that mission could have foreseen the freak explosion that endangered the lives of the three astronauts on board the Apollo 13 spacecraft. None of them could have thought to prepare for something like that. But even though they couldn't be prepared for that specific disaster, the NASA engineers had everything they needed to bring those astronauts home. Using their mental resources – intelligence, creativity, and problem-solving abilities – the NASA engineers were able to concoct a contraption out of duct tape, plastic bags, and cardboard that the astronauts could duplicate on board their spacecraft, and that provided them with the oxygen they needed to stay alive. Think of it: duct tape, plastic bags, and cardboard. I love the can-do scrappiness of that.

The engineers didn't spend months, weeks, or even days, worrying about an unlikely explosion that might incapacitate the spacecraft. But when the moment came, they were prepared, mentally, to deal with it.

I'm thinking maybe the best way to "prepare for the worst" is to spend our time being fully alert to what's happening in this moment - open to all the possibilities of good, recognizing and accepting good when it appears to us, and aware of the infinite resources around us. Maybe the best way to prepare for the worst is to expect the best. (It might be helpful to always bring duct tape with you, too.)

It is the end of my second year at the alternative high school now. Things are winding down here. My seniors are getting ready to graduate. Yesterday my last student gave her Culminating Project PowerPoint presentation. She did a great job. After her presentation the director of our school asked Rosa what the best part of going to this school was for her. Rosa answered, "My teacher. She is the best teacher I've ever had. I love her." She started wiping the tears from her eyes, and laughing at herself at the same time.

I was tearing up, too, of course. "I love you, too, sweetie," I told her.

And that – right there – that moment and moments like it – that is why I teach.

I'm so grateful I was led to leave the old for the new – to let Love "make all things new" in my life. If I hadn't been willing to leave the old job I wouldn't have found the new job, and I wouldn't have been able to work with Rosa and all my other amazing students.

You remember those happy golfers I mentioned at the beginning of the book? I still have a ways to go to get to where they were, but I think I'm getting closer.

I was wondering what we should write in the Bible," said Dorcas, looking at Jerry inquiringly. "I know what to write," Simon declared. "I've seen it written in a book before. It's the proper thing to write in a book. Daddy has a book with that written in it and he said it made the book more valuable— that's what Daddy said." "What is it?" asked Jerry and Dorcas with one accord. "With the author's compliments," said Simon proudly.

- D.E. Stevenson

"Now mud lies down again and goes to sleep. What memories for mud to have! What interesting other kinds of sitting-up mud I met! I loved everything I saw! Good night."

- Kurt Vonnegut

Made in the USA
Middletown, DE
29 September 2015